GUIDE

to
Supplier
Relationship
Management

in the Supply Chain

Stuart Emmett

Printed and bound in the United Kingdom by
4edge Ltd, 7a Eldon Way Industrial Estate, Hockley, Essex,
SS5 4AD.

About this book

Our *Excellence in...* series, covering topics like Leadership, Management, Purchasing/Procurement, Warehousing, Freight Transport, Supplier Management and Supply Chain Management have coverage of between 60 000 and 80 000 words per title.

However, to complement this larger series with some extracts that distil the essence of key areas within these topics, we have started to produce a series of 'Quick Guides' which will be 20 000 to 30000 words.

This first Quick Guide, on Supplier Relationship Management, covers one subset of Supply Chain philosophy.

Supplier Relationship Management (SRM) has evolved, like much of the left or upstream side of supply chain management, from cloning marketing approaches in the demand or downstream right side of the supply chain.

Following from the marketing approaches to customer categorisations with product segmentation (for example, The Boston Box, or the BCG Matrix), these approaches to customer categorisations that have more recently been readjusted and reappeared in procurement as Category Management. Customer Relationship Management (CRM) has also now come over to the supply side as SRM; although unfortunately this has caused much confusion – for example SRM can be presented as merely a database of suppliers with software program analysis and data manipulation.

Whilst we will discuss this confusion later, for us SRM is all about collaborative relationships that require, amongst many things, trust. Whilst this "T" word may be relatively easy to define, trust is often difficult to "design into" people so that trust becomes an effective part of an organisation's structures and processes.

We therefore define Supplier Relationship Management as being:

"A holistic discipline to work collaboratively, with those suppliers who are vital to our success, by maximising the value of our relationship where such a vision for me, must also be viability for you."

One thing is sure, and this will be discussed more fully later, SRM in this book is most definitely not treated as a computer software program which manages a database of supplier transactions. In many ways SRM is a shift of perspective and a change in the way an organisation works with suppliers; it is far more than doing new things with new people and/or, spending money on new software tools.

SRM must become rooted in an individual's personal software (or whatever we wish to choose to call, the brain, our beliefs or the thinking that creates our personal action and behaviour) which will then work through people into the design of organisational structures and processes and "the way we do things around here".

It is very clear to many, that working with others in a better way really does work; as SRM is proven to give mutual benefit and that elusive "win/win". But to get to this nirvana requires a paradigm change to our thinking and the consequent way that things are done. This is not always going to be easy, but just as with many groundbreaking approaches, it is only the adopters who finally get to receive the benefits.

We have therefore presented many case studies in this book that provide evidence of such benefits. Indeed we devote around half of this book to case studies, which also demonstrate the practicality of SRM, provide encouragement and prevent a purely academic or theoretical view of SRM.

In this regard, it is important to realise that relationships are a foundational necessity for any effective working with people, whether this with personal relationships or inter-personal relationships at work or non work; this is because relationships and trust are indelibly connected. If there is no trust, then there is no effective relationship.

Finally, we sincerely hope this book will inspire you with SRM in your organisation; after all:

"Managing a dependent process in isolation and managing it independently is plain folly. Managing the supply chain without the collaboration of the other players is a fruitless strategy."

– Emmett and Crocker, 2006

In writing this book, I have endeavoured not to include anything that if used, would be injurious or cause financial loss to the user. It must be appreciated that legislation, rules and regulations change – the user is therefore strongly recommended before applying or using any of the contents, to check and verify their own organisation policy/requirements. No liability will be accepted by the author for the use of any of the contents.

It can also happen in a lifetime of learning and meeting people, that the original source of an idea or information has been forgotten. If we have omitted in this book to give anyone due credit, we apologise and hope they will make contact so we can correct the omission in future editions.

This book is intended for:
- Leaders who wish to take their followers forward and create new team collaborative structures
- Managers in all procurement and supply roles and positions.
- Academics such as lecturers or students studying business topics like procurement, purchasing and the supply chain
- Students of professional institutes such as the Chartered Institute of Purchasing and Supply, The Chartered Institute of Logistics and Transport, Chartered Management Institute and the Institute of Leadership & Management and others.

About the Author: Stuart Emmett

My journey to today, whilst an individual one, did not happen without the involvement of other people. On this journey of lifelong learning and meeting people, the original source of an idea or information may have been forgotten. If I have omitted in this book to give anyone credit they are due, I apologise and hope they will contact me so we can correct the omission in hopefully, a future edition.

To all those who had contact with me please be assured you will have contributed to my learning, growing and developing. If you ask me how, then I will tell you! Whilst thanking you all, my hope is that I have given something positive back to you. I am pleased to acknowledge that my learning still continues; indeed writing this book has certainly contributed to my learning and development.

I have a background in freight, warehousing, shipping, and international trade and have resided in both the UK and in Nigeria. Since 1998 I have been an independent mentor/coach, trainer and consultant trading under the name of Learn and Change Limited. I currently enjoy working all over the UK and on four other continents, principally in Africa and the Middle East, but also in the Far East and South America.

Additional to undertaking training, I have been involved with one to one coaching/mentoring, consulting, writing, and assessing along with examining for professional institutes' qualifications and as an external MSc examiner.

I'm married to the lovely Christine, and have two adult children, Jill and James; James is married to Mairead. We are additionally the grandparents of three girls (the totally gorgeous Megan, Molly and Niamh).

More about me can always be found out by visiting my website: www.learnandchange.com. I welcome any comments.

Other titles by Stuart Emmett

Supply Chain in 90 minutes (2005), Excellence in Warehouse Management (2005), Excellence in Supply Chain Management

(2008), Excellence in Freight Transport (2009), and a series of seven Business Improvement Toolkits (2008) with individual titles on motivation, learning, personal development, customer service, communications, systems thinking and teams.

The following books were written in collaboration with other authors:
The Relationship Driven Supply Chain (2006), Excellence in Inventory Management (2007), Excellence in Procurement (2008), Excellence in Supplier Management (2009), Excellence in Services Procurement (2010), Green Supply Chains – an Action Manifesto (2010), Excellence in Global Supply Chain Management (2010), Excellence in Maintenance Management (2011), Excellence in Leadership and Management (2011) and Excellence in Public Sector Procurement (2011).

An Introduction to Supplier Relationship Management (SRM)

The Supply Chain fundamentally involves working with others; therefore also fundamentally, relationships (and their effective management) are involved. Two definitions of Supply Chain Management reveal this importance:

- "Coordination of all parties involved in delivering the combination of inputs, outputs or outcomes that will meet a specified requirement."
  (Supply Chain Management in Public Sector Procurement – a Guide, *OGC*, June 2006)

- "A network of organisations that are involved, through upstream and downstream relationships, in the different processes and activities that produce value in the form of products and services in the hands of the ultimate consumer." (Christopher, 1998)

As "coordination of all parties" and a "network of organisations" are the prime words used in these definitions, we can see a simple aim of supply chain management must be one that will integrate, coordinate and control the whole supply chain. This is perhaps well known and accepted, but what is not commonly accepted, is that this integration and coordination also be within "the hearts and minds of people."

Whilst the use of technical tools, systems and techniques do enable supply chain management, these must not be used in isolation from people and relationships. As noted by Peter Drucker, "because the object of management is a human community held together by the work bond for a common purpose, management always deals with the nature of man."

Therefore to manage the supply chain effectively, we must look to people to bring in collaborative relationships both internally (between the people processes and structures), and externally (between organisations with different people, processes and structures). As we have noted on collaboration elsewhere:

Collaboration is:
- Selective dialogue between the "right" people
- Intense and focused with investments of time/resources, of the whole organisation
- Taking the long term and strategic view
- To improve the performance of the whole supply chain

Collaboration is not:
- A SRM software package
- 'I will take all the benefits"
- A quick fix
- Easy
- For everyone
- A "one size fits all" approach

(Emmett and Crocker, 2006)

Indeed, collaboration is the supply chain. Effective collaboration is also a pre-requisite to prevent any one sided power plays (for example between buyers and suppliers), which are often then accompanied by short term gains for one party. However, these are often destined for longer term failure, simply because of the lack of engagement in enabling and releasing the total value that could be available from the other parties in the supply chain.

Much of the discussion so far is on organisational behaviour, which traditionally, mirrors and flows out from the organisations culture and structure. Here we can often find blame and adversarial communications taking place within functional silos, where these silos, are independently managed with accompanied internal politics and power plays. However, it is irrefutable that the simple reality should be one of interdependence (and not independence), yet, it is still all too common to find inconsistent access to information, isolated functional only reporting, built in conflict and overall, minimal levels of internal and external collaboration.

The theme of this book therefore, is to suggest changing such a status quo and, to do this, organisations will need to develop:

- End-to-end approaches to their culture (for example, by using a share to gain approach).
- End-to-end approaches to their processes and structure (for example, by having cross functional elements).

Additionally, as Professor Allan Waller noted, "we have been taught to compete, not to cooperate", therefore we need to replace competition by cooperation. This is analogous to having effective team playing where people with different skills work together, to achieve a clear and commonly accepted goal. Taking a collaborative view also requires an understanding that the suppliers have a view of us, after all "perception is reality" and we really will need to know how suppliers view us. We would ask here that you think over the following quadrant models overleaf:

Suppliers' view of buyers

High account attraction

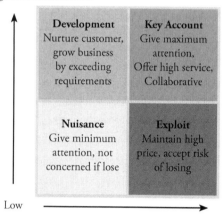

Low

High profit potential

Supplier objectives

High account attraction

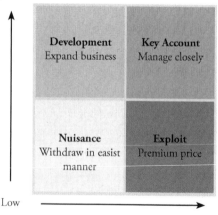

Low

High profit potential

The high account attraction will cover the suppliers' views of what they can get from a customer, such as:

4

- Opportunities
- Potential for growth
- References/prestige
- Relationships
- Reliability, for example, on time payments
- Responsiveness, for example, in handling problems
- Resilience, for example, in for the long term ("stick-ability")
- Low risk customer

Whilst we have covered this topic fully in *Excellence in Supplier Management* (Emmett & Crocker, 2009), buyers will ignore at their peril the ramifications of the above views, and must also totally dismiss any views that they are, automatically, a key account for all their suppliers.

It should also be appreciated that collaboration applies to all of the parts and all of the players in the supply chain. Whilst a major aspect of this book concerns supplier relationship management, there is also the requirement to work closely with customers, for after all, it is ultimately the demand from customers/consumers that drives the whole supply chain.

Therefore "Partnership with our suppliers enables us to share demand data to improve product availability and successfully bring new products to market; partnership with our customers allows us to better understand their needs and provide a tailored end-to-end solution to their needs."

(See Construction and Wolseley supply chain Case Study in the appendix)

Essentially therefore, SRM is one attempt to combat adversarial seller/buyer relationships and considers instead the use, as and where appropriate, of collaborative relationships. An overview of the differences in such relationships is shown in the following table:

	Adversary	Collaborative
Measurements	Used as a weapon One way feedback	Used for improvements Shared feedback
Procurement processes	Prescriptive specifications Close book/fixed price Passive suppliers	Performance specifications Open book Active suppliers
Time scales	Short term contracts	Long term contracts
Behaviour	"Me" Closed, aggressive	"We" Open, sharing, trusting
Attitudes	Reactive to change	Proactive change

As already noted, collaboration is the supply chain, however it also represents far more than this:

"In the long history of humankind (and animal kind, too) those who learned to collaborate and improvise most effectively have prevailed."
– *Charles Darwin*

Supply Chain Strategy and Tactics

Collaborative relationships in Supply Chain Management (SCM) must have a strategic view that sees that the supply chain networks extend both upstream and downstream and that these networks are varied and complex, with many supplier/customer interactions and trade off opportunities. Additionally, this strategic view should recognise that; competitive advantage is only gained and the optimum cost/service balance is only ever found, with collaborative management of all of these network relationships.

6

This is the strategic future for supply chain management that additionally represents a philosophy and approach to use that will guide what needs to be done. Meanwhile, the tactical management of the supply chain will concentrate on those functional processes that will deliver the required levels of cost/service to meet the strategic plans. Here, there is the need to integrate/coordinate and control both the internal organisation and the external Suppliers/Customers; this being the tactical "implementation and doing" aspect of SCM.

Links to the supply chain rules

In an earlier work, we identified the following 8 Supply Chain Rules (Emmett, 2005), which illustrate in a concise way just what Supply Chain Management is about. We therefore reproduce a summary of those rules here, with the collaborative and relationship aspects highlighted:

Supply Chain Rule number 1: "Win the home games first". This is all about changing the **internal workings to be collaborative** by removing silo functions and staffing the functions with "T" shaped people, who still have the functional depth, but have gained cross functionalism.

Supply Chain Rule number 2: The format of inventory and where it is held is of common interest to all supply chain players and must be **jointly investigated and examined**.

Supply Chain rule number 3: The optimum cost/service balance will only ever be found by **working and collaborating fully** with all players in the Supply Chain, starting internally (see rule number 1) and also externally with suppliers and customers.

Supply chain rule number 4: Time is cash, cash flow is critical and so is the goods and information flows; **fixed reliable lead times** being more important than the length of the lead time.

Supply Chain Rule number 5: The Customer is the business; it is their demand that drives the whole supply chain; therefore **finding out what customers value** and then delivering it, is critical.

Supply Chain rule number 6: It is only the movement to the customer that adds the ultimate value; **smooth continuous flow** movements are preferable. The movement to the customer, undertaken as quickly as possible whilst accounting for the associated cost levels, is really all that counts in adding value. The ultimate value is only found from the customer.

Supply Chain rule number 7: Trade off by **looking, holistically,** with all, the supply chain players; stop incrementalism and **get the whole supply chain working together**.

Supply Chain Rule number 8: Information flows lubricate the supply chain; therefore using the appropriate ICT is critical.

Five of these rules have collaborative and relationship aspects directly mentioned, in the other three, this will also be needed, for example; lead times improvements involve working better with external suppliers; movement flows to the customer involve many of the supply chain players as also do, the information flows.

Indeed whilst the Supply Chain is certainly driven by the flows of materials and the flows of information and money, in our view, we should critically also have people working together in flow; that special state when people are connected and think together; when there is a positive relationship with no separation; when people (and organisations) are connected by "hearts and minds".

This will involve some large supply chain players having to recognise that "just because you happen to be the biggest link in the chain, this does not imply superiority". (*A UK Car Assemblers* Case Study in the appendix).

We therefore must find ways to "unleash all of the individual talent and then weld it together". (T*he Partnership Sourcing* Case Study in the appendix).

It is only by doing this, that supply chain success can be finally realised.

2 | Supplier Relationship Management in Practice

Supplier Relationship Management (SRM) involves changing from a basic buying process of managing supplies, to one that extends to managing suppliers. Subtle word changes, but this often is a profound difference, not just in the practices and applications but mainly in requiring a new paradigm shift in thinking. Perhaps the greatest barrier in some cases, is the reality of paradigm paralysis; this being the inability or refusal to see beyond the current models of thinking.

SRM will for example, involve changing from having supplier meetings dominated by "yesterdays" contract/service issues (often conducted in an adversarial and competitive manner), and more towards changing working with suppliers by firstly concentrating on how best to work together collaboratively; this involving a process of continually solving problems and driving towards organisational learning that challenges people to grow.

Taking a longer term view of adding value, effective SRM will then move away from a cost emphasis (as this can effectively exclude, obtaining extra value) and also moves away from any short-term saving approaches that become eroded over time.

SRM recognises "Business is increasingly interdependent, where action takes place between and not within" (Emmett and Crocker, 2006) and therefore aims for increasing service from suppliers by removing animosity in customer/supplier relationships, for example:

> "Let's work together to find the best way to improve service and reduce costs."
> (*Collaboration and Proctor and Gamble* Case Study in the appendix)

"There is no option but to move quality up and take suppliers along with you. The endless search for the lowest price simply does not work and has comprehensively been proved to be wrong." (*Partnership Sourcing* case study in the appendix)

"Key suppliers work collaboratively, ensuring efficient processing and best practices, driving out competitive edge." (*Institute of Business Ethics Report*, 2006)

There is a lot of evidence that SRM been well practiced for many years, and whilst we have many longer case studies in the Appendix, here we would briefly mention the following examples:

Case Study | Toyota

Toyota's view of suppliers is:
- Suppliers are seen as "extensions"
- Selected with care (as is done with our own staff/personnel selection)
- Developing suppliers (as done with our own staff)
- Use a long term partnership approach
- Tier structure with levels of responsibility
- Set up strict cost targets and timing e.g. expect 3-4% price reduction per year
- Integrate methods/systems (e.g. on JIT, NPD)

Toyota supplier partnering involves:
- Mutual understanding
- Trust

- Commitment to co-prosperity
- Respect for each other's capability
- "GOYA" (Get off your ass") and "Go and see and talk and listen"

Interlocking structures
- Alliance structure
- Parallel sourcing
- Interdependent processes

Control systems with
- Measurements
- Feedback
- Target pricing

Compatible capabilities
- Engineering excellence
- Operational excellence
- Problem solving skills

Information sharing
- Accurate data collection and dissemination
- Common language
- Timely communications

Joint improvement activities
- Value added and value engineering
- Supplier development
- Study groups

Case Study

Dutton Engineering UK in the 1990s

"Suppliers as Partners" initiative

- Apply TQM principles
- Philosophy of trust and empowerment
- Teamwork widely used, including with suppliers and customers
- Supply base of key partnerships (had 80% of materials from 12 suppliers)
- Aim: to minimum total acquisition cost (TAC) with, maximum service

Methods used

- Held a supplier day with an agenda of:
  - Explained TQM, e.g. involve all employees, proactive to continuous improvement, cooperation and teamwork
  - Suppliers invited were told they were to be single sources
- Future to be based on
  - Openness/trust
  - Clear joint objectives
  - Long term view with no year-end re-negotiations

Basis of supplier selection was

- Culture of TQM 30%
- Quality 25%
- On time delivery 25%
- Price 20% (Total Acquisition Cost or TAC is used as this "is more than the price on the invoice")

Approach of "Partners as suppliers"
- Trust implicitly e.g. no inspection
- Kanban supply e.g. two bin, suppliers call in once/twice a week, no orders are placed
- Some non Kanban by team leaders with a single PO
- Reduce non value added e.g. no delivery notes, invoice once per month e.g. goods as listed on computer disk, e.g. Purchase Orders down by 80%
- Reduce TAC e.g. suppliers offload delivery vehicles, joint design of packaging

Benefits
- For Dutton
- ✔ Secure supply
- ✔ Reliability in delivery
- ✔ Improved quality
- ✔ Purchase administration was reduced to 20% of what was done before
- ✔ Reducing TAC
- ✔ Growing sales
- ✔ Lead onto outsourcing of transport, cleaning, gardening and some "standard" manufacturing with own plant kept for prototypes and small runs
- For Suppliers
- ✔ Long term, so can plan forward
- ✔ Freedom to perform
- ✔ Paid on time
- ✔ Financial stability

(Focus, CILT magazine, February 1996)

Case Study

A contrast in UK experience in the 2000s

National Stadium at Wembley, London
- Design-and-build contract.
- Fixed-price, lump-sum.
- All risk is passed to the contractor as "we protect against failure".
- Labour and people problems.
- Opened in March 2007, almost a year late.
- Over budget.
- Lots of litigation.

Heathrow's Terminal 5, London
- Work in partnership with contractors. Contract required totally integrated teams, including the principal subcontractors, through main contractors and designers to the operator (BAA) and the end user (BA).
- Contractors are paid on a cost-reimbursable basis, with performance bonuses.
- Risk is accepted by BAA as "we have a hared interest in successful outcomes".
- Opened on time in March 2008.
- On budget.
- "T5 people always talk about the contract; it's what everything we do here is based on. Usually in this business, the contract tells you what to do when things go wrong, but our contract tells you what to do to make things go right".
- "We took in our suppliers as partners and got them involved at a much earlier stage than is normally the case.

> - Usually in this business there is a complete break between the consultants who design the things and the contractors who build them-there is no meeting of minds.
> - Note, we explore the above two cases later in this book.

The above excellent examples of collaborative relationships from recent decades are however, sadly today, the exception rather than the rule. Why is this? Why do we have few successful widespread SRM implementations, yet the proven benefits are visible?

Some possible reasons follow:

- a lack of knowledge of what SRM is and what the benefits are
- a lack of knowledge on where and how to start
- a failure to learn and change the thinking
- a failure in implementing change with a preference to stay "rowing the boat we know"

We will be exploring these reasons more fully shortly, but suffice to say in the meantime, reasons can also be, unfortunately, because of the lack of clarity and meaning in the words supplier relationship management.

SRM is all too commonly, and confusingly, seen as a software program. For example, the main ERP supplier SAP advertises its supplier relationship management software as covering the integrated source-to-pay process and that its SAP SRM application automates, simplifies and accelerates procure-to-pay processes for goods and services. Whilst there is no doubt this is a valuable offering, SRM is very much more than a standard purchasing cycle or procure to pay (P2P) procurement process.

Additionally with such procurement software programs and systems, it has been well noted by Alan Day that "a number of organisations reported confusion among internal stakeholders as a result of transactional procurement modules in their ERP systems being badged as SRM".

Clarifying SRM definitions

We have already defined supplier relationship management as follows:

> "SRM is an holistic discipline to work collaboratively, with those suppliers who are vital to our success, by maximising the value of our relationship where such a vision for me, must also be viability for you".

The main points here, are that whilst buyers certainly need to ask the question, "Can this supplier improve the way we work and compete", by remaining with a one (my) sided view, the tendency here is actually towards seeing SRM as being only the monitoring and improving of the suppliers' performance. However, a question is also, "Why should the supplier choose to engage?"– this because SRM must be seen as a two-way, beneficial process.

The UK Chartered Institute of Purchasing and Supply (CIPS) usefully encapsulate these points in its definition of SRM as being the "process for managing the interaction between two entities, one of which is supplying things to the other entity. SRM is a two-way process in that it should improve the performance of both the buying organisation as well as the supplying organisation and hence be mutually beneficial. It involves proactively developing relationships with particular suppliers".

As an indication of what is important in SRM, research shows that it is the behavioural aspects that are around 70/80% of implementing a full SRM program, whereas, the technical aspects, such as software tools, are only some 20/30% of such a change. This is really critical and in our view explains much of the failure in understanding and applying SRM.

Having such a correct reality of the need to concentrate on the behavioural aspects, is therefore critical and interestingly, also counters those who believe the main way to make the change is to use only technical-based tools and techniques (such as only by using software programs).

For example, as the Senior Supply Chain Manager of a well known Global MNC said during a training course about introducing SRM, "we do not want any soft skills being talked about, we just want the tools". A wrong view, as the principle fact in SRM, is that the behavioural soft skills aspects must "rule" and must be the prime focus to enable a successful introduction.

Additionally, whilst conducting a three day course on Supplier Relationships for a major UK utility who had recently outsourced all of their basic engineering work, a delegate was absent for half a day, attending a meeting with their main contractor; effectively, a very key supplier. When he returned and was asked how the meeting had gone, his answer was "we gave them a bloody nose." Such a comment revealed their old style adversarial approach with suppliers, but fortunately and helpfully, one other delegate suggested "that comment represents the problem we have to overcome in ourselves".

The above two examples show the difficulty that can result in introducing SRM. It is good to have a vision and strategy for SRM, but without a correct understanding of what is involved, followed on by an effective implementation, then, as with many strategic initiatives, we can find failure on implementation. (It is because of this poor implementation reality, that there is a clear step by step approach in the appendix on how to plan and implement a SRM programme).

SRM Reported Barriers

If we look at some evidence of poor relationships, then the following issues have been identified:

- High administration costs
- Time spend price wrangling
- Time spent resolving problems
- Too many meetings with too many people
- Unwilling to consider simple solutions to problems
- An atmosphere that discourages innovation
  (*Toyota in Institute of Business Ethics*, Supplier Relationships report 2006)

Another view follows to show the barriers that must be overcome.

 Barriers to managing
Supplier relationships
(*IJLR&A* Volume 14, number 3 dated June 2010)

Mainly Strategic leadership issues

- Lack of vision e.g. unclear picture of benefits
- Lack of formal Supply Chain strategy e.g. how to internally integrate all of the supply chain internal and external processes
- Lack of proper planning e.g. internal and external performance planning
- Lack of leadership commitment e.g. top management support is a prerequisite to achieve SC benefits, along with a thorough concentration on the fundamentals, rather than an over preoccupation with the "latest" new thing
- Seeing SCM as a buzzword/"flavour of the month" e.g. job titles/departments are changed to use the words "Supply Chain" but nothing else changes

Mainly Structure and Management issues

- Lack of training, especially for executives e.g. people are promoted from operational functions with a lack of ideas on how to leverage technology, on the use of finance and little understanding of implementing strategy; all of which are needed to handle the new complexities and achieve the required supply chain benefits
- Failure to communicate e.g. do not communicate supply chain issues in ways that can be understood either by top management or by functional managers
- Functional silos and no common goals e.g. no joined up process thinking (as retain a preference to "stay in the box")
- Focus on short term and tactical issues e.g. ignore the requirement for the long term build up of close cooperation with suppliers, as prefer to concentrate on short term cost-cutting

Mainly Buyer/Supplier relationship issues

- Insufficient communication between supply chain players e.g. follows from a lack of using common goal approaches, so, do not see any need for information sharing
- Reluctance to share knowledge and learning between supply chain players e.g. follows from lack of trust, cultural differences, etc.
- Lack of confidentiality e.g. lack of trust, information sharing, blame and not gain approaches, etc
- Traditional procurement methods that use "arms length" approaches e.g. power based views of arms length

adversarial and tender procedures limit collaboration along with resistance to change that takes time, patience and training to overcome.

- Limited interest from suppliers e.g. it cannot be assumed a supplier will be automatically interested

Therefore it seems for success that we need to have:
- Strategic Vision
- Formal strategies
- Proper planning
- Leadership commitment

Mainly Structure and Management issues
- Training
- Communication
- Removal of functional silos
- Common goals
- Focus on long term issues

Mainly Buyer/Supplier relationship issues
- Better communication between supply chain players
- Shared knowledge and learning between supply chain players
- Confidentiality arrangements
- Collaborative procurement methods
- Interest from suppliers

SRM Benefits

Using the above mentioned Institute of Business Ethics, Supplier Relationships report, it could be simply argued that the benefits of an effective SRM program are the opposites, such as:

- Lower administration costs
- Little time spent on price wrangling
- Less time spent resolving problems
- Fewer meetings
- A willingness to consider simple solutions to problems
- An atmosphere that encourages innovation

Improvements from using SRM will often focus on the "normal usual suspects" of any Supply Chain Management improvement program, such as the following:

- Demand forecast sharing
- Order lead times
- Inventory status sharing
- Inventory reductions
- Shipment sizes
- Shipment frequency
- Supplier lead times
- On time delivery
- Joint KPIs
- Packaging

However with an SRM program, the following should also be evident results:

- Improved relationships, especially with more effective talking and listening.
- Innovation in products and processes.
- Joint problem solving and preventation becomes routine
- Sharing development costs, for example, in new designs of products/services and the subsequent marketing etc.
- Reduced cost/risk, for example, capital expenditure and competitive pressures.
- Increased efficiency/quality/service, for example, the time

to market for new products/services.
- Developing trust and having committed people, for example; "I fundamentally disagree with the way this sector views its people as a commodity that is easy come and easy go. We treat people differently here and so we get something different back." (see the Terminal 5 case study in appendix).
- Overall, working together to make it easier to do business together.

Trust

A bottom line in changing relationships will always involve trust, that "something" we know of when it is not here, but with which we have difficulty in defining, and difficulty in knowing just how to get it.

Trust however remains something of a "touchy-feely" concept for many organisations, which is why many have find it difficult to get to grips with as it is always easier to talk about more concrete topics, such as profit and performance. Yet trust is actually quantifiable as the following shows:

> "Trust is not something soft and fluffy. The absence of trust has a direct impact on the bottom line. It affects financials and the business performance. You ignore it at your peril:' (*People Management*, 22 February 2007)

> "Trust is not a soft 'nice to have' quality; it is quantifiable, hard, real and measurably affects both speed and cost." (Stephen Covey, *The Speed of Trust*)

Trust remains the critical aspect when dealing with relationships and three levels of trust have been usefully identified:

Trust Level 1: Contractual and "Service": Boundary time bound trust for standard performance, with data exchanged for transactional trading.

Trust Level 2: Competence and "Satisfaction": Reliable trust for satisfactory performance, with some information sharing and cooperation.

Trust Level 3: Commitment and "Success": Goodwill open ended trust giving beyond expectations success with, cognitive connected decision making.

– Dr. Mari Sako

The attendant differences and benefits as trust progresses through these levels can be clearly seen.

A consortium of business leaders worked on leadership and trust and came to several conclusions, with arguably the most important being that trust is akin to a currency by building up a healthy deposit account which is essential so that withdrawals can be made when something goes wrong.

Trust has also been seen as creating three types of value for an organisation:

- The stock price is influenced by investor/analyst trust in the management team
- Customers trust the organisation's brand and reputation
- Employees are willing to offer discretionary effort if they trust the organisation will reciprocate.

Organisational trust also needs to endure beyond the personalities of the individuals, who will inevitably come and go. It needs to be embedded in the organisation as "the way things are done around here"; in other words, it must be in the cultural DNA of the organisation and encourages co-operative behaviour, information sharing and personal risk-taking. More thoughts on trust in practice follow:

"It changes the paradigm. It's definitely a different type of relationship with your customer. It's based on mutual trust and it's got to be there to succeed."

"On paper, the process seems simple to implement, but in the real world of personalities and professional relationships, there are many obstacles to climb. Trust is very important for success."

"You can define any relationship by the degree of trust. No trust, then no relationship. This applies both in business and also in personal life."

"The biggest thing my boss could do for me is to trust me."

3 | Supplier Service

Organisations are now well versed in customer service, indeed the customer is the business for many. This was not always true but now there is the acceptance of the importance of customer service is well recognised (if not always well practiced).

At the other extreme, conceptually, from customers, we have suppliers and as supplier service is a concept very similar to customer service, then it may be usefully considered to give a view of SRM. Suppler Service presents some interesting and possibly controversial views, and perhaps in time, may become as well recognised and important as the customer side.

Our contention here is a simple one: suppliers are critical in delivering customer service, as if there is no supplier, then there is no service for customers. Let us amplify further the importance of supplier service.

The supply chain is also the supply-demand chain and also the supplier-customer chain. The supply chain can also be visualised as a series of connected links of suppliers and customers:

S: Suppliers
C: Customers

There are many and multiple supplier/customer connections in any supply chain. Such connections can be internal or external ones, involving internal departments in an organisation, or, external suppliers or customers. For example; the passing on of paperwork to the next person, the passing on of a sub assembly on an assembly line or, the supply of component part from an external supplier.

Of course, and to state the obvious, suppliers have customers and customers have suppliers and additionally, one maybe a customer in one transaction, but are then a supplier in another transaction.

Suppliers will, naturally and normally, view the next connection link as a customer. However, rarely will customers view their suppliers in the same way as they do with their customers. Yet in the supply chain process, they are both connected dependently.

If buyers would see suppliers the same as they see their customers, then supply chain relationships should change and then, overall, the end service to the ultimate end customer should be "perfect."

This is therefore what we have called supplier service. Whilst we do not really want to add to the multitude of jargon that already exists in our profession, it is our belief that seeing suppliers in a similar way to how we already see customers will more readily bring in the required paradigm shift in our thinking on SRM and in dealing with suppliers; dealing with suppliers well, seems to be something the following organisations seem not to know how to do:

> "The *Mail on Sunday* alleges the Retailer was asking 700 of its suppliers for a contribution from their contracts and the company was to lengthen its payments terms from 60 to 90 days." (*Supply Management*, 18 January 2007)

> "The Company is locked in a bitter dispute battle with its suppliers over attempts to extract cost savings from its supply chain…One supplier claimed the company were arrogantly out of touch." (*Sunday Times,* 11 February 2007)

Seeing suppliers in the right way, however, will mean that the following rules and actions have to apply with suppliers:

Supplier
Service Rules

- Believe that suppliers possess good ideas.
- Gather supplier feedback at every opportunity.
- Focus on continual improvement.
- Actively solicit good and bad feedback.
- Don't spend vast sums of money doing it.
- Seek real-time feedback.
- Make it easy for suppliers to provide feedback.
- Leverage technology to aid your efforts.
- Share supplier's feedback throughout the organisation.
- Use feedback to make changes quickly.

Definitions of Supplier Service
Supplier service can be seen in various ways, and the following five views represent some different definitions:

1. Supplier service is seen as a need satisfier
"Supplier Service is a function of how well an organisation meets the needs of its suppliers."

2. Supplier service is seen as taking care
"Supplier Service is a phrase that is used to describe the process of taking care of our suppliers in a positive manner."

3. Supplier service is seen as keeping promises
"Supplier Service is the ability to provide them with feedback in the way that it has been promised."

4. Supplier service is seen as adding value

"Supplier Service is a process for providing competitive advantage and adding benefits in order to maximize the total value."

"Supplier Service is the commitment to providing value added services to external and internal suppliers, including attitude knowledge, technical support and quality of service in a timely manner."

5. Supplier service is seen as all of the supplier contact

"Supplier Service is any contact between a supplier and a company, which causes a negative or positive perception by a supplier."

Supplier focussed procedures

Top leadership must therefore have the commitment to suppliers and implement supplier focussed procedures. What is important here to accept is that the supplier is:

- a part of the business
- an important person to have contact with
- one we depend on
- a human being with feelings and emotions
- not one to win arguments with, but someone who can help us to build our business and give us a competitive advantage

All suppliers will expect, as a minimum, the following:

- Reliability, for example, honesty and ethical approaches, not cancelling orders at short notice, etc.
- Responsiveness, for example, to requests, receiving payment on time etc.

- Accessibility, for example, to people who can help them.
- Accuracy, for example, in communications.

Providing suppliers with the above will prevent them from being dissatisfied; however these will not, by themselves, provide satisfaction. To provide supplier satisfaction, the following are required:

- Fully meet supplier's expectations (and therefore prevent dissatisfaction)
- Courtesy
- Empathy
- Provide exceptional quality
- Good people relationships
- Delivery of value
- Handle well any complaints
- Give them repeat business

Supplier Perception and Attitudes

One of the obvious difficulties in meeting supplier's expectations is that "Perception is Reality." Therefore, we are entering again into human variability and subjectivity. Everything that is done for suppliers, will be the supplier's perception, and how they perceive it, is real to them. A buyer's reality should therefore be the supplier's perception of the buyer's performance. Many people, however, are uncomfortable with this "reality check" and see it as an unsolvable dichotomy in whatever "normal" buying is supposed to be.

However, one very clear reality (one often not recognised), is that a person's attitudes and feelings will definitely affect the way any service delivery is perceived. Accepting this view will require some flexibility from management, such as giving discretion to staff to

31

deal with suppliers and not only relying on any standard and fixed structural procedural manuals and guidelines.

After all, suppliers are individuals and therefore, organisational procedures must support this. Service is all about delivering not only what is the result of doing business with your organisation, but also with you personally. Feelings and attitudes are therefore an important aspect, please consider the following diagram:

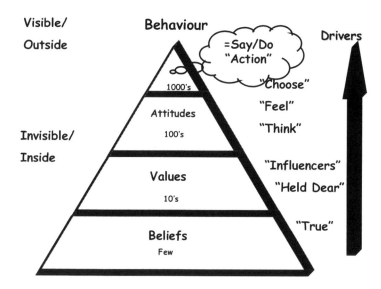

Our attitudes are underpinned by our beliefs, and values will work through into how we behave (defined here as what we say or do).

We will therefore tend to judge from our perspective alone and will not always consider the other parties fully enough.

Good supplier focussed people will therefore have a deep belief that supplier service is important, they will value this and will then lead by example, so that this belief, will then work through into their attitudes and be shown and reflected by what they say and what they do.

Good supplier focussed people will therefore:

32

- pull more than push
- be two-way communicators
- makes concessions: "I think this, but what do you think?"
- problem solve and explore interests
- hold views and reasons that "working together works"
- believe fully, the above is the best approach

Of course the opposite is also true and often when buyers report problems with suppliers, this can be because they do not have a belief that suppliers are important to them. As was said by Henry Ford, "If you think you can or think you cannot, you are right." Simple perhaps, but profound in its application and to changing what is done with suppliers. When our beliefs are impacted and changed, then many other changes will automatically result.

Supplier complaints
Common complaints from suppliers are when the following happens:

- Their expectations are not met; e.g. a change to promised order quantities or to agreed scheduled delivery times
- Inflexible responses has been received; e.g. when a procurement department (the only department the supplier has had contact with), makes a response to a delayed payment enquiry by saying, it is "nothing to do with me, check with the accounts department".
- Mistakes have been made; e.g. forgetting to say that something has changed.
- Communications are poor; e.g. a use of telling one way with no listening or checking for understanding
- Delays have been made in payment; e.g. cash flow is critical in all business and cash flow problems are a major source of company failure/bankruptcy, therefore unplanned

payment delays mean supplier cash flow problems. Where however these delays have been anticipated by suppliers, then suppliers may "compensate" by charging higher prices, reducing service levels, look for alternative customers or even withdraw from the business.

- Dealing with unprofessional people; e.g. "some buyers treat suppliers as if they dirt on their shoes" (a comment from a manufacturers trade association over buyers unilaterally increasing supplier payment terms).

Benefits of being a Supplier Service focussed organisation

To move towards being a supplier service focussed organisation, it is necessary to know:

- Who your suppliers are
- What they expect and need from you
- How well you are meeting their expectations
- How to provide supplier care and follow up
- What needs to be done to make improvements
- What the barriers are to making these improvements
- How you can remove these barriers

The following shows the differences between supplier-focussed and non-supplier focussed businesses, and what is important:

Supplier service focus	Non supplier focus
Profit comes from supplier and customer satisfaction	Profit comes first, then supplier and customer satisfaction
Preventing problems	Detecting problems
Explicit standards	Vague standards

Complaints are seen as a chance to learn	Complaints are a nuisance
Run by people working with other people using systems, if appropriate	Runs by systems and procedures and then people

A supplier service focussed organisation will therefore have the following five key attributes:

- Reliability: Dependable, accurate performance consistently and in all of the details.
- Ownership: Front line ownership, so that those who receive complaints are also able to sort them out.
- Responsiveness: Clear evidence of a willingness to help.
- Attitudes: Courtesy, friendly, empathy and caring by employees for the suppliers "unique" requirements.
- Appearance: Clean and tidy facilities, equipments, people etc.

Benefits

As has been seen, the road to improving supplier service may not be easy; however the benefits can be huge and long-lasting. The following benefits will all make contributions to the survival, well-being and the profitability of any organisation:

- Reliable service with a marketable product with a price difference.
- Market changes that can now be better handled and managed.
- Continuous improvement becomes a part of the culture, with innovative and responsive staff.

35

- A positive view of your organisation from shareholders, the community and potential employees.
- Competitors who "fear" your organisation.

Suppliers who now see the organisation as being:
- responsive and listening
- collaborative and sharing
- understanding what is critical to their own success
- "good people to deal with"

The way suppliers are handled is therefore fundamental – the following will give another view on this.

Supplier Approaches
The following questionnaire can be asked to give an indication on the approaches that are being used with suppliers:

A simple supplier approach questionnaire
Score: 1 to 10 as follows:
1= totally agree with list A
5=neither
10=totally agree with list B

	List A	List B	Score
Suppliers are called	Vendors	Partners	
Approach with suppliers	"Attack/Defend"	Collaborative and problem solving.	
Dependency	Independent	Inter-dependence	

Risk	All is externalised to suppliers	Shared and open	
Outcome	Self survival	Mutual survival	
Controls	KPIs are used for control and compliance actions.	Mutual agreed KPIs, discussions on shortfalls and remedial actions.	
Contracts	Legal contracts	Moral agreements	
		Score: From 7 to 70=	

Score Explanation

7 to 34: List A favoured: Combative/Competitive approach
35 totally neutral
36-70: List B favoured: Collaborative approach

To change the approach/ways forward:

- understand the current position
- understand the gap between where we are and want to be
- understand what drives the differences in the two positions
- understand to change from the current "Status Quo" will require change to beliefs and values and attitudes and behaviour
- create an action plan, for example the 4 step model in the appendix

Finally on supplier service, the following checklist gives more ideas on dealing with suppliers from using the view that buyers are the suppliers' customers:

Ten golden rules for becoming an attractive customer:

1. Be a demanding customer.
Challenge your suppliers, but don't crush them. If hard-hitting negotiation is the only tool in your bag, you have problems. Attraction does pay off, but you need to check opinions with key suppliers: Do they see you as only pushing prices?

2. Determine which suppliers are important.
Attraction is not to be spread around like so much peanut butter. Identify which partnerships will pay off in the long term, and invest in them.

3. Recognize, explicitly, that attraction is double-edged.
You will need to work hard to be seen as your key supplier's most attractive customer. This also implies joint improvement efforts, not unilateral demands for the supplier to make them.

4. Increase the supplier's comfort level.
Make sure that supplier managers know their ideas are welcomed, acknowledged, and implemented. Make it easy for them to provide them. Be fair and scrupulously honour contractual obligations.

5. Help the supplier properly evaluate its expected payoffs.
A typical negotiation technique is to hide information. In fact, keeping information from key suppliers leads to poor evaluation and diminished attraction, of both customer and supplier.

6. Manage the misalignment.

It is virtually impossible to align the objectives of purchasing, manufacturing, R&D, finance, and other functions. It is even more critical to understand and manage misalignment between the partners.

7. Manage the perceptions.

Understand that it is perceptions that matter, and that these are often totally unrelated to reality. Proactively manage the "stories" and "feelings" about a supplier.

8. Understand and manage how the supplier allocates resources and ideas. Develop the reputation of being the most open customer to new ideas, by accepting as many ideas as possible and implementing them. Develop metrics that support implementing supplier ideas, and reward those in your company who do so.

9. Help your suppliers leverage the learning.

If you not only allow but deeply encourage your suppliers to use the learning with their other customers, you will increase attraction and be the place where new learning is focused.

10. Sell the opportunities in your company to the supplier, and understand which other customers and initiatives are in the priority list of the supplier. You want to be at the top of it.

(Carlos Cordon and Thomas E. Vollmann, 2008, *The Power of Two*)

4 The Three Supply Chain roles

Following from the earlier discussion on supplier service, we can conclude that each organisation has three main roles in supply chains – namely as a:

- Supplier
- Customer
- Value creator

With the first two roles, we need to see the connections and the mutual effects both of these roles have. For example, as we have just explored above, what would change if we were to see suppliers in the same way that we view customers?

As has also been shown, some of the most important principles of supplier service are exactly the same as customer service principles, for example:

- Suppliers (and customers) have needs and expectations.
- Supplier (and customer) service can be a source of competitive advantage.
- Supplier (and customer) service is always delivered by people, so how they do it, is more important than what the product/service being delivered actually is.
- Supplier (and customers) offer different levels of service.

The third role in supply chains of being a value creator, is where each party in the supply chain, is able to create value. However it is useful to realise that this is going to come more from "those who really know how to do things; the suppliers and specialist contractors" (see the *2005 Contracting* Case Study in the appendix).

Such value creation has two main aspects:

- Value is found when something; satisfies a need, conformed to expectations and/or, gives "pride of ownership", i.e. it is "valued" over something that is not. Here then the perception of value will differ and maybe value is, simply, what the customer says it is; where customers will have different perceptions of "worth" and "price." For example, different customers have different perceptions of quality/ lead time and the cost/service balance. Maybe therefore, value can be seen at the balance/pivot points between worth and price, between quality and lead time and between cost and service?

- Value is also the opposite to cost and in many supply chain processes, more time is actually spent on adding cost instead of adding value. A business would not find it worthwhile to invest and automate wasteful non value added activities as waste is the symptom, rather than the root cause of the problem. Attention should therefore be actually given to those activities that do add "real" value, for example:

  - ✔ Make it faster, through, form changes (e.g. redesign a product).
  - ✔ Move it faster, through, times changes(e.g. shorten the transit time).
  - ✔ Get paid faster, through, place changes (e.g. sell Ex Works).
  - ✔ Serving the customer better.

A supply chain view of added value would also recognise that it is only the movement to the customer that is adding (the ultimate) value. Stopping or delaying the flow, adds costs. It is only the movement to the customer that adds the ultimate value; therefore, smooth continuous flow movements must therefore be preferable.

Value and competitive advantage

Supply chains as well as individual organisations compete, and increasingly it is the supply chain that brings competitive advantage for many organisations. In turn, competitive advantage can be seen as being a cost leader or a service/value leader; as shown by the following comparison where the former is essentially represented by a lean supply chain and the latter by an agile supply chain.

Cost Leadership – give same standard products/service at a lower price "Do it cheaper" and Waste minimised, or being "Lean"	Product or Service Leader – give products or services that can't be found anywhere else. "Do it better" with Value added (being "Agile")
Standard products	Customer designed product/ services
Standard offering	Value added bespoke offering
Production push Flow and mass volume production, with high mechanisation	Market pull Job shop production with low mechanisation
Low inventory levels	Flexible inventory
Focus on productivity and efficiency	Focus on creativity and innovation
Stable planning	Flexible planning
Lowest possible costs with service a constraint	Maximises innovation responses/service with cost a constraint
Lead time reduction	Short lead times/quick responses
Minimise waste	Maximise service

These two positions can be expanded as follows, where it is possible, if not easy in practice, to offer both cost and service/value leadership.

Competitive advantage

Differentiation

	Product or Service Leader = Value adde, or Agile	Cost and Value Leader
	Commodity	Cost Leadership = Lean

High ↑

Low ————————————→ High

Cost advantage

Value creation and suppliers

The challenges to be faced in value creation will basically involve doing things faster, for example, making products quicker, moving them into the marketplace faster and also, getting paid faster.

The attendant supplier involvement, on the basis of product quality and reliability in lead time and delivery performance, will therefore, be required. This means facing up to challenges such as:

- Reducing inventory.
- Responsive order processing.
- Short and reliable last times; this is not just the supplier lead time, it is the overall supply lead time from all those involved in all processes from the start to the end (or, from the initial need to being available for use).
- Product received is the "right quantity, right quality, at the right time and the right cost".
- Using appropriate ICT.
- Close working relationships and the understanding of all the supply chain "players".

44

This focuses, for a specific supply chain, onto all of the current material and information lead times, the storage/static times and the payment/credit times; as well as the associated customer service requirements of availability, delivery schedules/frequencies and the requirement to provide customers/users with continuous reliability over a long time period.

How well all of these aspects are managed will actually affect profit and a business strategy. Suppliers are also connected into this value creation, as shown in the following diagram.

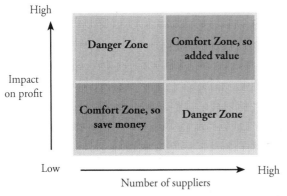

Clearly therefore, the view must be that suppliers should be consciously and better joined up to their client's business. This must be more actively considered by many organisations, so that the links between suppliers and customer service will then be better managed, for example where, "we took in our suppliers as partners and got them involved at a much earlier stage the is normally the case" (see the *Heathrow Terminal 5* Case Study in appendix).

Value, relationships and exchanges
Adding value and value creation is rarely going to be achieved by single views or by one party. As we have shown above, value creation is two-way involving all parties making choices in how they can work together by consciously deciding what type of relationship is

required, and what needs to be exchanged between each party.

Exchanges here being anything that is exchanged between suppliers and buyers/users/customers so that value is created for mutual benefit, for example exchanges of:

- People, e.g. on secondments, job swaps etc.
- Materials, e.g. designs, joint procurement.
- Plant and equipment, e.g. sharing.
- Money, e.g. loans, investments.
- Information, e.g. patents, real time access to each others systems .
- Methods of work e.g. ideas, different ways.

Looking at the short and long term positions of value creation related to relationships and exchanges, such connections can be seen as follows:

Need for relationship

The varied positions from the above matrix can be amplified in the following table:

Position	Need for relationship	Need for exchanges	Comments	Procurement Portfolio (Kraljic) examples
Transactional	Low	Low	Each party having separate main goals and are only together for a short term deal	Routine and leverage items.
Exclusive	Low	High	Needs some specific exclusive exchange for only a short time	New product launch.
Cooperative	High	Low	Working together is needed to secure supply, but there is little need for exchanges	Bottleneck items.
Collaborative	High	High	Both parties are in it for mutual gain and have open access to each others resources	Critical items.

As already noted, adding value and value creation is rarely going to be achieved by just the one party and requires suppliers to be connected with customers/users/buyers. Where there is any dissatisfaction, then this needs working at, unless of course, power plays are in force that prevents this happening. If such power plays do happen, then possibly full value creation, will be prevented.

Accordingly making such relationship connections will have the view that suppliers are like "cogs in the machine" and cannot be viewed as being "easily replaceable." Additionally, replacement suppliers may not be available and when losing a supplier, this may well be at the "knock on" cost of lost sales and lost customers. Harnessing the supplier's knowledge can therefore add value to both organisations.

Aligning Suppliers and Customers

If we look at the 5 Rights of Purchasing (quality, quantity, time, place, price) and connect and relate this across to the Kraljic procurement portfolio (see *Excellence in Procurement,* 2008, for a more detailed discussion on Kraljic), then we can see buyers actually have the hierarchy of requirements shown below:

The Right	Bottleneck/critical items Aim: Secure supply and therefore lower the risk for non-supply	Routine/leverage items Aim: Reduce price by playing the market, possible outsourcing etc.
Quality	Secondary	Secondary
Quantity	Secondary	Secondary
Time	Number one	Secondary
Place	Secondary	Secondary
Cost	Secondary, maybe last	Number one

On a cost/service and supply balance from the buyers/customers and demand perspective, then the following is indicated:

- Bottleneck/critical items have service requirements/ KPIs first, especially the lead time on delivery, with the cost KPIs secondary,
- Routine/leverage items have cost price requirement/KPIs first and the service aspects KPIs are secondary.

49

The matching response related to Kraljic, from the supplier's and supply perspective of what the customer wants, is then going to be as follows:

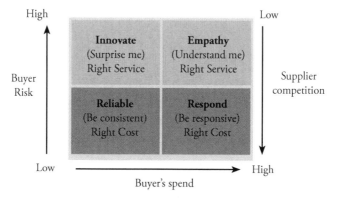

The above can be amplified in the following table:

Service winner	Buyers Strategy	Matching Supplier Behaviour	Suppliers Market position
Responsive	Leverage items with Supplier Sourcing "Plays the market"	React rationally with price cuts	Certainty of competition in the short and long term
Reliability	Routine items with Supplier Outsourcing "Organises and lets go"	React by exploring options and "fit"	Certainty of competition, in the short term, followed by stability in the long term

Innovative	Bottleneck items with Supplier Development "Secures supply and attempts to diversify"	Proactive entrepreneurial behaviour with new product designs, or, Reactive positions when maintaining the monopoly	Uncertainties of being able to innovate, high R&D costs, followed by possible monopolistic position
Empathetic	Critical items with Supplier Collaboration "Work collaboratively with suppliers"	Proactive team work and problem solving	Uncertainty initially (forming-storming) followed by long term performing

The question to be asked here is, will the above-mentioned supplier behaviours line up with the buyer's strategy? If there is congruence, there is agreement and progress forward will be made as both buyer and supplier will have their needs met.

If there is no congruence, then whilst there are possible negotiations options and positions may change, the outcome can be an eventual "no deal". Clearly the appropriate behaviours by either party affect the supplier/buyer relationship. This is easy to understand – after all, 'what you sow, you will reap'.

Interpersonal behaviour in the supply chain

The above discussion also shows us the common and continuing organisational problem; the underpinning inter-personal behaviour of the people involved – such individual people being the suppliers/sellers/buyers/users and customers, who may also actually do some things for their own reasons and not necessarily in line with what the employing organisation expects.

This is briefly explored below and it will be seen that this can cause "interference," as what is actually going on, may be different, to what was expected or planned to happen.

- **Leverage buying and responsive supplying** takes us to toward the transactional/adversary buying behaviours that requires, as a service winner from suppliers, their rational response. The logical and stable thinking patterns revealed here are more of a logical left brain approach. Providing this happens then there is good fit.

- **Routine buying and reliability supplying** is also more towards the transactional/adversary buying behaviour and requires as a service winner from suppliers, a response that explores options and of continually sensing for a "fit". The suppliers perhaps using exploratory and innovative thinking patterns; this being a creative right brain approach. This may however conflict with the buyer's view of seeking a rational logical response. However, the supplier cannot likely give this, until they have explored more creative options; a possible "no meeting of minds" here.

- **Bottleneck buying and innovative supplying** is more towards exploratory buying approaches that requires service supply winners of intuition and exploration and eventual product change .This creativity also requires a more right brain supplier approach and if buyers do approach suppliers this way, then there is a good fit. However where the sellers wish to maintain any supply monopoly, then they will here be displaying more rational and logical left brain behaviour.

- **Critical buying and empathetic supplying** approaches require collaborative responses involving both logical thinking and emotional feelings; a typical combined right and left brain approach. This is however difficult for many individuals to use and apply; hence a team approach can be used here to give a more effective balance with both logical and emotional traits introduced which is then used as and when appropriate.

The following summarises these varied views against the appropriate brain sides of left (more logical and competitive) and right (more emotional and cooperative).

Buyers' view	Buyer brain side	Seller brain side	Sellers' view
Leverage	Left	Left	Responsive
Routine	Left	Right	Reliability
Bottleneck	Right	Right, but possible left	Innovative
Critical	Left and right	Left and right	Empathetic

Clearly again here, whilst this is an ideal typical model, it can be appreciated which are the more appropriate brain sides that are needed; but bear in mind, "one size does not fit all." For success, approaches that recognise these varied and applicable options must be considered.

The SRM Challenges
As well as potential incompatibility in interpersonal behaviour, there can be many other challenges when introducing a SRM program and following our earlier discussions, we identify for example:
- No trust.
- Poor communications.
- No "big picture" view.
- No risk taking.
- Preference for the power based adversary transactional approach where for example: "The most powerful is seen as wielding the biggest stick".
- Wanting quick and short term wins.

- No sharing of benefits.
- No planning.
- No support for any changing "how we do things".
- "Output is king here and anyway, we are too busy fire-fighting".
- Fear of change.
- Fear of failure from the existing blame culture.
- Convincing the significant stakeholders.

This shows again many of the challenges with the first one recognising, that a major barrier is the lack of trust. There are many ways this can be "outworked", for example, built up historical mistrust can remain and also, the difficulties in sharing information, where information is seen as power, leading onto a reluctance to relinquish power and therefore, to actually share any information.

We can refer back here to earlier comments from research on SRM implementation that indicates it is the behavioural aspects that are 70/80% of such a change, whereas, the technical aspects, such as ICT software, are 20/30%.

It is rarely easy to change "the way we have always done things around here" and therefore careful consideration is needed to ensure that a programme is not lightly started. Additionally abandoning a program too easily is also dangerous, as it destroys any creditability and belief. A program should also never begin unless senior management supports it fully and openly and matches actions and words. There also needs to be an expectation of eventual success and to publicise the success steps along the way.

It will help to anticipate problems by ensuring that more time is made available in the early days along with extra management resources. Open communication is needed with good exchange of information which involves listening before acting and being able to receive and accept criticism. Above all, commitment and will from all who are trying to succeed to make change happen.

Whilst all of these challenges are further covered in the 4 step model to SRM in the appendix, when change is involved, then other considerations are needed.

Change as a paradigm shift

If we look at what has changed in recent decades, we can identify the following:

The past normal and status quo	The emerging new status quo
Factory model with cheap and plentiful standard products for a mass market	Craft inventive model with bespoke products for a "fashion" driven economy
Manager as the main technical expert.	All are experts, for example everyone has two jobs, one as per the job description, the other, to improve it.
Behaviourism with reward/punishment.	Empowerment
Central and bureaucratic control	Organic, self and fluid controls
Brain is mainly seen as being logical, for example, IQ testing only	Brain is also seen as being emotional, for example, the "birth" of emotional intelligence and EQ profiling
Narrow local problems with local, perhaps national solutions	Wide global problems requiring holistic solutions
Cost reduction	Service/value for money enhancements with Total Cost analysis
Competitive approaches	Collaborative approaches

The point here is that the process of change itself is not new, but as we know from some of the above examples, change has been and is commonly resisted; however, to eventually enable such changes, this meant that people had to change their thinking and acquire different perspectives.

Making such changes may of course, be uncomfortable. For example, some would agree that "Trust is the emotional glue that involves commitment to others" whereas some others would say, "Emotions have no part to play in business". So how can we change our thinking?

Well no easy one size fits all answer, but it helps to see that our thinking comes from our mental maps that are like computer programmes and give us our own personal predetermined actions. For example, our attitudes/beliefs/values, will work through to give us our "reality" and resultant patterns of behaviour.

Whilst with computer programmes we must check and re-calibrate the parameters (for example, with inventory systems where supply lead time is usually not a constant), the question to be honestly and personally answered here is, how often do we challenge our own mental map parameters?

People working together in flow

As has been noted, "As a person thinks, so they are" and "If you think you can or think you cannot, you are right".

The way a person thinks, therefore creates their immediate world view and determines how they work together with others, and then in turn through to the collective of people in organisations. Ultimately, such influences will guide and shape the organisation and its relationships with others.

Indeed, we can actually identify the following types of organisations from looking at the left and right side brain divisions of people.

"The Left Brain Organisation"	"The Right Brain Organisation"
Short term results	Long term success
Problems reoccur as only the symptoms are treated; ("Band aid" solutions)	Problems are tackled by looking at the cause/thinking
Rational and Silo thinking using mainly Science and Technology	Emotional and Holistic thinking with Motivating/ Empowering people
"Facts" and "the numbers speak for themselves"	"Solutions" and "it is how we connect that is important"
Follows existing and known ways	Experimentation

The Left Brain organisational type clearly presents an obstacle to effective SRM and as noted earlier, research indicates that behavioural aspects are around 70/80% of making the change needed, whereas, technical aspects are only some 20/30% of change.

Really capturing hold of this reality is critical and counters those who still believe the main way to make the change are to use only technical based tools and techniques. These can assist, but they are not the most important and will not enable effective change and SRM practice. As noted by Jan Carlzon in *Moments of Truth* (1987):

"Running a business is not always a matter of logic and mathematics. It is just as much a question of understanding the psychological impact."

Let's always remember that the Supply Chain is driven by flows of materials, information and money, but it also needs people working together in flow – that special state when we are connected and think together; when we have a positive relationship with no separation; when we have connected our "hearts and minds". Only then, can we realise supply chain success.

"Incremental change is not good enough; you have to get people to think differently." (see the *Heathrow Terminal 5* Case Study in appendix).

Making changes may not be easy, especially when it requires changing something that has worked well in the past, but the main difficulty is with changing embedded thinking. Therefore, as noted before with SRM, "you have to handle it with care", to get, "a benefit of shared knowledge and experience which benefits everyone, particularly your customers." (see *A Car Assembler's supply strategy* Case Study in the appendix). Some final views or lessons from experience follow:

"Benefits of our Collaboration programme include:
- Improved service levels.
- Faster flow of product through the supply chain.
- Rational use of resources and more effective promotion planning.
- Synchronisation of production to better match supply with demand.
- Shared responsibility and mutual trust"
  – *UK FMCG Retailer and Supplier*

"A real focus on joint and collaborative planning has been critical. It's all very well putting in great capability and structurally changing our supply chain, but at the end of the day, you can't make it happen unless you work together."
– *Logistics Manager*, June 2004

"Collaboration will be the critical business competency of the

internet age. It won't be the ability to fiercely compete, but the ability to lovingly cooperate that will determine success."
– James M. Kouzes, *The Leadership Challenge*

"Coming together is a beginning. Keeping together is progress. Working together is success."
– Henry Ford

Hopefully few will by now need convincing that a collaborative business relationship extracts mutual benefit from having long-term, high value commercial transactions, where collaborating simply means helping each other to derive more value. Without doubt, effective collaborative business relationships facilitate the creation of business value to mutual benefit; this is re-emphasised below:

"Because the focus of relationship management is on the business relationship between the two trading parties, the maximisation of the mutual business benefits for the parties is its prime concern. It follows therefore that relationship management should drive the relationship between the parties, rather than contract management or delivery management, although both of these latter two functions have supporting roles to play in assisting and informing the relationship management function. So in short, relationship management puts the 'collaboration' into collaborative business relationships, ably supported by contract management and delivery management".
– What Drives Collaboration in Collaborative Business Relationships, by Ian Deeks (Ten Squared Limited) in *IACCM Contracting Excellence,* 24 February 2011.

Finally, in the Appendices, we look at models for introducing and implementing SRM and improving supplier relationships, along some more practical examples of collaboration in the UK.

Appendices

Appendix 1: Case studies on some of the history from 1990 of UK Supply chain collaboration

In more recent years the UK has a good record of looking into supply chain relationships and varied studies and reports have been published. A summary of these works follows, after these; we then have a series of organisational experiences.

1990: Partnership Sourcing Ltd

PSL was established by the Confederation of British Industry (CBI) and the Department of Trade and Industry (DTI) in 1990 to promote the concept of partnering in business. Soon after its formation, PSL produced a video, which makes the following points. Aim of partnership sourcing: total customer satisfaction with increased quality and reduced costs.

The natural world has many partnerships where we find working together to give collective achievement for greater gain, whereas, if they were only to use individual effort, then they would get less.

With buying/selling, adversarial approaches rule with short term power plays to get a lower price and "good enough" quality. In the medium term, this is mutually damaging and also nationally, erodes wealth creation. In a global village, countries must be internationally competitive. We need partnership sourcing, to unleash all of the individual talent and then weld it together.

Examples:

- Japanese in 30 years dominated car production and changed from mass to lean production. Dan Jones comments that this involves: shared interdependent destiny, long term goals, work together to improve, clear rules, e.g. profit share, therefore you have to be rewarded if you take part. Suppliers are equal partners in a long term relationship

- Marks & Spencer have shared commitment, openness, as they see confrontation brings only a short term gain
- Unipart went to Japan in a "leap of faith", started small, now they are the sole supplier of catalyst converters to Honda UK. Have mutual trust at all levels, and, Unipart can invest with confidence
- Guinness suppliers made technical innovation (widget in cans), suppliers gain from rolling long term forecasts, and cost increases are absorbed by savings elsewhere
- McLaren – relationships are founded on trust as no longer circle each other to see the strengths and weakness. Is constructive but equally is destructive if trust is broken
- Partnership sourcing is fundamentally needed but it needs "change" towards a more secure future. John Neill of Unipart says there is no option but to move quality up and take suppliers along with you. The endless search for the lowest price simply does not work and has comprehensibly been proved to be wrong.
- PSL still continues its work – and has now changed its name to the Institute of Collaborative Working – find more at http://www.instituteforcollaborativeworking.com/

Since 1990, the following Key UK reports have been published:
- 1992 Oil and Gas CRINE Report
- 1998 Construction Report
- 1998 The Audit Commission
- 2002 LOGIC and Project Supply Chains
- 2002 Oil and Gas Code of Practice
- 2003 Housing: the evidence

- 2004/5 Construction: the evidence

We look at each of these below:

1992 Offshore Engineering and CRINE

In 1992, the UK offshore oil and gas engineering industry in the North Sea faced a crisis when the price of oil dropped to from $35 to $12 a barrel, making exploration uneconomic. Platform operators, contractors and suppliers came together to form the Cost Reduction Initiative for the New Era or CRINE; a cooperative effort to find ways of reducing wasteful activity in platform construction.

After 12 months of investigation and analysis the CRINE Report was published, recommending:
- functional rather than prescriptive specifications'
- common working practices
- non-adversarial contracts
- use of alliances
- reduction in bureaucracy
- a single industry body for pre-qualification

These recommendations were put into practice by industry. As a result the cost of oil and gas developments was reduced by 40%.

An unexpected result was the emergence of a network of innovative individuals committed to on-going co-operation for further improvement. By 1997 CRINE had been transformed into the CRINE Network, a continuous agent for change and a brand-name for cost reduction and competitiveness in the oil industry. Its vision is "People working together to make the UK oil and gas industry competitive anywhere in the world by the year 2000."

CRINE remains a model of "co-operative effort" in the supply chain which has been emulated and copied in many parts of the world. It has usefully been extended, through the ACTIVE Engineering Construction Initiative to the UK's process plant industries, with a view to improving efficiency and enhancing competitiveness.

– *Rethinking Construction, 1998*

In 1999 CRINE moved into LOGIC (Leading Oil and Gas Industry Competitiveness) set up by the Government's Oil and Gas Industry Task Force to improve competitiveness by targeting efficiencies in the supply chain.

LOGIC is a not-for-profit, wholly-owned subsidiary of Oil & Gas UK. LOGIC owns the "intellectual property rights" to the cross-industry projects mentioned above and acts as their custodian to preserve their unfettered availability, and to promote and develop their use to improve industry practice.

See: http://www.logic-oil.com, and also 2002 below.

1998 Construction Industry and the Supply Chain

The Underlying Principles:

- Compete through offering superior value rather than lower margins
- Establish long term relations with key suppliers
- Manage the supply chain during a project through supply clusters
- Make "value" explicit: design to meet a functional requirement for a through life cost
- Involve the supply chain in design and cost development- using target costing, value management and risk management
- Develop continuous improvement within the supply chain
- Promote collaboration through leadership, facilitation, training and incentives
  – Prime Contractor Handbook of Supply Chain Management, March 1999

1998 – A Fruitful Partnership: effective partnership working: The Audit Commission

The Audit Commission use the term 'partnership' to describe a joint

working arrangement where the partners:
- are otherwise independent bodies;
- agree to co to achieve a common goat;
- create a new organisational structure or process to achieve this goal, separate from their own organisations;
- a plan and implement a jointly agreed programme, of-ten with joint staff or resources;
- a share relevant information; and
- pool risks and rewards

The key points are:

Deciding to go into partnership

1. Does this organisation have clear and sound reasons for being involved in its current partnerships?

2. Where new partnerships must be set up to meet national requirements, what groundwork is being done locally to maximise their chances of success?

3. Are changes in behaviour or in decision-making processes needed to avoid setting up partnerships with only limited chances of success?

Getting started

4. Have all the partnerships in which the organisation is involved been reviewed to evaluate whether the form of the partnership is appropriate to its functions and objectives?

5. Do all the partnerships have an appropriately structured board or other decision-making forum?

6. When setting up a new partnership, how are prospective partners identified?

Operating efficiently and effectively

7. Do partners share the same main objectives for the partnership?

8. Are the partnership's objectives consistent with those of the partnership organisation?

9. If an outsider watched a partnership operate, would they be able to identify the partnership's main objectives?

10. Do the partners know where the boundaries between the activities of the partnership and of their own organisations lie?

11. Do the members of partnership steering groups have sufficient authority to commit their organisations to decisions?

12. Are partnerships prepared to delegate responsibility for parts of their work to particular partners?

13. Do large partnerships have an executive group that all the partners trust to make decisions on their behalf?

14. Are project-planning techniques used to ensure the separate agreement of all the partners to a course of action in good time, when necessary?

15. Do the partnership's decisions get implemented effectively?

16. Are partnership staff selected for their technical competence and for their ability to operate both inside and outside a conventional public sector framework?

17. What actions are taken to build and maintain trust between partners?

18. If members have dropped out of a partnership, what lessons have been learnt about how to maintain involvement in the future?

Reviewing success

19. Does each partnership have a shared understanding of the outcomes that it expects to achieve, both in the short and longer term?

20. What means have been identified for measuring the partnership's progress towards expected outcomes and the health of the partnership itself?

21. Has the partnership identified its own performance indicators and set jointly agreed targets for these?

22. Are the costs of the partnership known, including indirect and opportunity costs?

23. Are these costs actively monitored and weighed against the benefits that the partnership delivers?

24. What steps have been taken to make sure that partnerships are accountable to the individual partners, external stakeholders, service users and the public at large?

25. Are some or all of the partnership's meetings open to the public?

26. Is information about the partnership's spending, activities and results available to the public?

27. Does the partnership review its corporate governance arrangements?

28. Has the partnership considered when its work is likely to be complete, and how it will end/handover its work when this point is reached?

– *The Audit Commission: A Fruitful Partnership: effective partnership working*, 1998

2002 LOGIC and Project Supply Chains
What's it about?

World-class performance in offshore projects has been achieved in very few instances and will continue to do so unless there is a shift in mindset and performance.

Key to success will be a company's ability to control the costs of its products and services while increasing the value it delivers to its client.

Longer supply chains will mean more dependence on other companies and so collaboration throughout the project supply chain is becoming a must as opposed to traditional adversarial relationships. Indeed, competitive advantage is increasingly coming out of the ability to challenge assumptions.

Introduction

Subcontracting has increased in today's project business due to the trend of companies specialising and focusing on their core competencies. Supply chains become thus longer and longer. In order to manage the chain and achieve the chain's major objective, the final customer's satisfaction, it is essential to understand the concept of project supply chain as a whole.

Definition of "project supply chain"

Project supply chain is the global network used to deliver a project from raw materials to the final project customer through an engineered flow of information and physical distribution.

Points to be highlighted in this definition are the global network and flow of information. Stressing the importance of the global network is necessary because most often the other companies in the project supply chain are not located locally but on another continent. Most companies in the oil and gas industry work in global markets and also have global networks of suppliers involved in the projects. Also, pointing out that the supply chain is not only for the distribution of the physical products, but also for the distribution of all the related information, is necessary.

Most of the problems in project supply chains are caused by communication problems. The interfaces of successive phases in the supply chains have not been clearly defined, which has lead to disruptions, cost over-runs and dissatisfied end customers.

These are not the only symptoms that results from the problems in the project supply chain, but it gives a hint of the underlying troubles.

Based on LOGIC's engagement with a number of companies working on different projects, a summary of the typical problems in the design to build project supply chains is illustrated in the figure opposite.

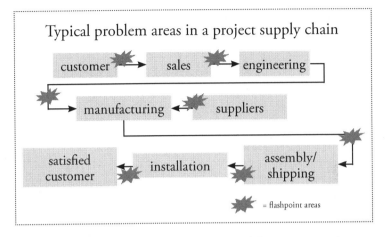

Problems are divided along the project delivery process line to emphasise that they exist at the interfaces between different units, and what is more important, at every interface.

The conventional approach in the offshore industry has been to use project management. The management of time, cost and quality drives this function.

However, consideration of these factors alone is not considered adequate to ensure the satisfactory performance. The design and build of offshore facilities poses difficult management problems to which the models and techniques based on the traditional project management view have proven inadequate. Trade-offs between competing design criteria must be made through the design process, often with incomplete information and under intense budget and schedule pressure. The use of project management alone has not proven capable of solving these difficult problems as illustrated by the number of offshore projects delivered late.

The traditional way of thinking about and managing offshore projects was formed in the 'good old days' when each phase was performed sequentially. The designer produced the design, including equipment and material specifications. Equipment and materials were purchased and delivered to the fabrication site. The fabrication contractor assembled the equipment and materials into the desired facility in accordance with the drawings and specifications from the designer. This non-overlapping sequence encouraged the misconception that each phase could be considered separately, without regards to interdependencies and trade-offs. The shift to concurrent design, procurement and construction strains the assumptions of independence, especially because of the obvious need to integrate the processes of each phase within a single unified supply chain.

The model for understanding the interdependency of these processes is what LOGIC calls "project supply chain". At its essence, an integrated project supply chain ensures that the right information and materials are, sent to the right parties at the right time. Projects participants share one guiding objective, to finish the work on time and on budget. Whether they build complex topside or subsea facilities, customers and project teams demand predictability and accountability first and foremost. How you manage the project supply chain can make or break a project.

By focusing on your project supply chains, you can minimise your organisation's total cost while growing business profitability and customer satisfaction. Enhancing supply chain performance through speed, focus and customer intensity will enable your company to realise your vision and business strategies ahead of your competition. The only relevant question in a project supply chain is how the participants in the supply chain can unite to create greater value for the end consumer and do it at lower total costs."

An outline of a presentation from LOGIC follows:

Project:
Nightmare conditions

- Lack of integration within team
- Poor communications between team members
- Lack of consensus within team
- Lack of understanding of each other's roles and constraints
- No knowledge of manufacturing constraints
- Lack of understanding of supplier capability
- Lack of planning and preparation
- Lack of understanding of customers underlying requirements
- Lack of parallel working
- Lack of work sharing
- Late placement of parts orders
- Ordered wrong parts/missed parts
- Too many parts in the product
- Dissatisfied customer
- De-motivated suppliers

What would make a project a success?
- A smooth and continuous flow of products and services
- Managed end-to-end
- A good contract
- Active Executive Sponsor/Project Sponsor
- Quality and value added at every step
- Good relationships and communication
- Improving performance
- Delivered within budget
- Delivered on time

- Satisfied customers
- Pro-active suppliers
- Shared risk and reward

Projects need help to make a Mindset shift…

Today	Aspects	Tomorrow
Functional organisation	Management framework	Empowered process owner
Guess or assumed	Customer requirements	Rigorously deployed
Secrecy and/or adversarial based	Customer/supplier relationships	Collaborative relationships
Individual task by function	Resource management	Cross functional task teams
Activity based (CPA)	Planning	Goal driven (consensus)
Test analyse and fix	Development	Simulation and design of experiments

See: http://www.logic-oil.com/projects/supplychain/index.html

2002: Oil and Gas: The Supply Chain Code of Practice

This outlines a set of best practice guidelines for the UK oil and gas industry to:

- Improve performance
- Eliminate unnecessary costs
- Add value and boost competitiveness

First adopted by the industry in 2002, signatories undertake to work towards full compliance. They include major purchasers (Oil and Gas operators and principal contractors) and suppliers (companies providing goods or services).

The Code applies to three key stages within the commercial process:

1. Plan

Transparent planning of contracting activity by major purchasers to improve supply chain capability

Major purchasers

- Communicate forward plans to the industry including areas and types of activity, expected contract value and timing.
- Support the annual industry Share Fair where major purchasers communicate future plans and internal contacts to the Supply Chain.
- Publicise a list of internal contacts to facilitate discussion around future plans with the contracting community.
- Maintain up-to-date First Point Assessment Limited (FPAL) Purchaser Profile including "how to do business with us" guidance, a contacts list and information on forward plans.

Suppliers

- Review Purchaser plans, FPAL Purchaser Profiles and attend Industry Share Fairs to understand future requirements.

2. Contract

Streamline pre-qualification, tendering and negotiation processes to reduce bidding costs, eliminate waste, add value and increase competitiveness

Major Purchasers

- Where pre-qualification data is required only invite bids from suppliers registered with FPAL with an up-to-date capability assessment.

- Eliminate supplier data duplication by utilising FPAL throughout the tender process.
- Use industry standard ITT Models where appropriate. These embody fair contracting principles, encourage participation, invite bidders to demonstrate where they can add value, define value-based award criteria, outline timeframes and avoid data duplication.
- Provide appropriate de-briefing for all bids.
- Use industry standard contract forms where available (LOGIC type or company-specific global contracts), minimising amendments or additional terms and conditions.
- Include payment terms of 30 days in all contracts.

Suppliers
- Keep FPAL records valid and up-to-date, with Capability Assessments where required by purchasers.
- Refer purchasers to FPAL if duplicate information is requested.
- Participate in the Industry Mutual Hold Harmless as appropriate to company activity.
- Use standard industry contracts (LOGIC type or company-specific global contracts) minimising amendments or additional terms and conditions.

3. Perform and Pay
Increase feedback dialogue and shorten payment cycles to improve performance

Major Purchasers
- Include performance indicators in all significant contracts with an appropriate review programme for the life of the contract.
- Give FPAL performance feedback at appropriate stages during the contract to improve mutual performance,

minimise waste, learn from mistakes and best practice, and report on the extent of Code compliance achieved by both parties.

- Pay all valid invoices within 30 days.

Suppliers

- Track and discuss key contract performance indicators
- Request and participate in FPAL performance feedback, including assessment of Purchasers' performance.
- Submit complete and valid invoices with supporting documentation in a timely manner.
- Adopt a prompt payment policy for own suppliers.

– www.pilottaskforce.co.uk

2003: Housing and Partnering Works

Old Procurement	New Procurement
Select lowest cost	Select on best value
Late involvement of key suppliers	Early supplier involvement
Defensive and confrontational contracts	Collaborate, cooperate, trust, honesty and sharing
Costly risk transfers leading to low profit margins	Open allocation of risks with auditable decisions and improved profits
High costs due to duplications, delays, disputes and defects (all are waste)	Time and cost savings without compromising quality
Poor H&S record	Improved H&S
Low rates of production/ construction	Shorter lead in times speeds production/construction

"Silo" working practices	Cooperation and longer term views foster training schemes and shared learning
No whole life costing	Focus on Asset management
Every contract is a steep new learning curve	Learning transferred from project to project and continuous improvements
Dissatisfied users/customers/ tenants	Increased satisfaction and wider community benefits

From: 'Partnering Works' in *The Housing Forum Report,* 2003

2004: Terminal 5 London Heathrow

The construction of Heathrow's fifth terminal is on time and to budget at its halfway point. It is as much to do with good people management as engineering process, says Andrew Saunders in Human Resources magazine November 2004 entitled, "Terminal Velocity".

Getting the builders in can be a traumatic experience, as anyone who has ever had an extension done or a new bathroom put in knows only too well. But if the prospect of having a gang of muddy-booted labourers loose about the house is enough to bring you out in a cold sweat, spare a thought for the BAA team. Their job it is to manage the 50,000 of them — from carpenters to civil engineers, roofers to electricians — who will, when Stage One opens in 2008, have built the new £4.2 billion fifth terminal at Heathrow Airport.

It's a historic project on a massive scale — the Richard Rogers Partnership- designed Terminal 5 (T5) is, on its own, larger than most European airports and will boost Heathrow's passenger capacity by around 50% to more than 90 million annually. Technically it's hugely challenging— simply preparing the 260- hectare site involved diverting two rivers. This was necessary before work could start on either the main terminal building, big enough to hold 10 football pitches on each of its five floors, or the secondary satellite building, itself bigger than the existing Terminal 4. Not to mention the 40,000-space car park or the 13.5 kilometres of new tunnels and an additional station required for extensions to the Heathrow Express and Piccadilly line transport links. And all the work had to be done on a site hemmed in by Europe's biggest airport on one side and its busiest motorway junction (the M4/M25 interchange) on the other.

With all that complexity, it wouldn't be surprising if technical hitches and unexpected hold-ups were destroying the timetable and stretching the purse strings. Unlike so many comparable high-profile construction projects, however, T5 is on time and on budget at its half way point. In a sector where huge delays and vast overspends are commonplace (the recently opened £40 million Scottish Parliament building was years late and cost 10 times the original estimate), this is something of a miracle. 'We've already broken records getting this far,' says Sharon Doherty, BAA's organisational effectiveness director for the project. 'If we were running to industry norms; T5 would cost another £1 billion and take 18 months longer to complete.

That they have done this well so far, says Doherty, is a tribute to innovative and people-focused working pr in an industry not known for progressive thinking. "I fundamentally disagree with the way this sector usually views its people - as a commodity that is easy come and easy go. People are generally not well treated, and of course this is part of the reason why so many big construction projects are late and over budget. We treat people differently here, and we get something different back.'

What that translates to in practice is better facilities for workers — decent canteens, air-conditioned site offices, a seven-person, on-site occupational health team and their very own award winning staff newspaper, The Site. Even minor details have been taken into consideration, such as well- organised parking and decent transport to and from work areas. It all helps to make the guys digging the holes in the ground feel valued, says Doherty.

This theme of better treatment giving rise to better results extends to he way BAA handles its key suppliers n T5, too. 'We took in our suppliers as partners and got them involved at a much earlier stage than is normally the case,' says T5's construction director, Andrew

Wolstenholme. 'Usually in this business there is a complete break between the consultants who design the things and the contractors who build them- there is no meeting of minds.

This can lead not only to design problems that could have been solved on the drawing-board, but also perpetuate is one of the fundamental structural problems in the industry. 'Contractors give low quotes to get the job and then win profit by forcing delays and overspends,' says Wolstenholme. 'But by integrating the design-and-build processes with our requirements, we avoid that adversarial system. If you took at what goes wrong with big construction projects, more than half problems are people issues.'

This brings us to the central plank of BAA's new way of working, "the Contract". Chat to anyone on T5 — from sharp-suited execs in the office to hard-hat and steel-toecap sporting contracting staff out on the site — and within a few minutes they all start talking about 'the contract". In most industries (and construction is no exception), this is normally a very bad sign. As a rule of thumb, people only start going over the paperwork when things have gone pear-shaped and they want to know whom they can blame. But not here.

'T5 people always talk about the contract, it's what everything we do here is based on,' says Wolstenholme. 'Usually in this business, the contract tells you what to do when things go wrong, but our contract tells you what to do to make things go right.' Perhaps the most singular aspect of it is the fact that BAA shoulders all the risk. It's a bold move that runs counter to standard procedure — partnership deals usually involve shared risk — but it works, says Wolstenholme. Freed of concerns over who takes the rap, contractors can concentrate instead on doing a good job.

This novel document has even got its own, uncontractual-sounding name, the T5 Agreement. Instead of portentous and vaguely threatening legalese designed to apportion blame and elicit compensation after problems arise, the T5 Agreement aims instead to forestall them by encouraging effective co-operation. 'The majority of it is about integrated teams and working well together, not dispute resolution says Wolstenholme.

He recalls a formative moment in his career, when working on the original Heathrow Express project in the 1990s. In mid-dig, the main tunnel collapsed and the team was left staring disaster in the face. If they had reacted in the usual way to such a calamity, he says, the tunnel would never have been finished on time. 'We would probably have been in a court of law well beyond the completion date.' Instead, they decide effectively to tear up the contract, opting instead for a more proactive approach, getting together with their contractors and solving the problem rather than apportioning the blame. It worked, the collapsed tunnel was rebuilt and the project was a success. It became the prototype for the T5 Agreement.

'Our contract actually states that we want different behaviours,' says Doherty. 'That gives me a hook for what I do, which is incredibly well-grounded in the business. Basically we behave with our suppliers as we would want them to behave with us, and create a problem-solving environment rather than a finger-pointing one.' If there's an issue or a potential delay— as arose recently with construction difficulties on the 87-metre high control tower called Hatchet, 'we all sit together round the table and come up with a solution'.

She concedes that it takes time for people who aren't used to working in this way to get the hang of it. 'People don't turn up here after 20 years of doing things one way and just get it. We have to show them what to do.' But she's been hugely impressed by the willingness of T5's key suppliers to make it work. 'I'm always amazed at how receptive they are. They are really trying to do the right thing. I'm not the HR director for 6,000 workers involved on this project, but I have to talk to the people who are and make them understand our standards. I can do that because of the relationships we have.'

Another traditional construction business headache to be addressed on T5 is the problem of waste. Contrary to normal procedure, where most of the assembly is done on site with all the dirt and risks of damage and delay that entails, '70% of our mechanical and electrical work is done off-site in a factory environment', says Wolstenholme, 'and delivered using the just-in-time principle. It's safer, more reliable and less prone to delays.'

For both BAA and its 60 or so key 'first-tier' suppliers it's a steep learning curve, but worth the effort. 'This is a historic project, reputations will be made by those working on T5,' says Doherty. Not to mention the fact that there's plenty more work to be done elsewhere, and those who acquit them selves well on T5 are likely to be closely involved in other parts of BAA's ongoing £8 billion programme at Heathrow, Gatwick and Stansted airports.

Employee engagement is the key to success, says Doherty. 'There are great people in this business, they have kids and families and they want to be part of something. They work hard, often away from home, and they have a choice. They can pitch up to work and not care, or they can pitch up and care about what they are doing. And that's what we do —persuade people to care, because in years to come they'll be standing here saying: "I did that"?

With a workforce that peaks at 6,000 at any given time and more than 400 supplier companies involved, that's a tough call. But T5's communications strategies help to get the job done, most notably the award-winning T5 monthly newspaper, The Site. Such is its popularity that it's the ideal means for communicating management objectives to staff in the most effective manner. True to its no-jargon ethos, the whole T5 strategy has been distilled into four statements which inform everything in the paper: to build T5 on time, on budget, to high quality standards and to do it all safely.

'This is an industry that has come to expect accidents, but I am passionate about safety,' says Wolstenholme. According to those construction norms again, as well as being late and over-budget, six people could be expected to die in the course of building T5. So far no one has died, and the whole team is determined to keep it that way, with an intensive safety programme for everyone on site. 'Incremental change is not good enough,' he adds. 'You have to get people to think differently about safety, to realise that if they can go home every day with all their fingers intact, that's a good thing.'

On grand projects like this one, it's all too easy for the huge technical dilemmas to overshadow the less dramatic but equally important aspects of success. That T5 is going to be ready for takeoff in 2008 is as much a tribute to good people management and communications as it is to engineering prowess. 'The vision for T5 is to be the world's most successful airport extension. For that to happen my goals have to be clear to those on the front line. Sharon's team plays a vital role in helping the senior management to think beyond the technical challenges; says Wolstenholme.

"The Contract"

TheT5 Agreement is central to everything that's good about Terminal 5. It is BAA's response to a project whose sheer size and complexity defy traditional construction management techniques. Legally binding, in essence it's a contract in reverse. Instead of specifying what redress can be taken in the event of things going wrong, it aims to stop problems happening in the first place. This is done by fostering constructive behaviour and a recrimination-free environment. Key features include:

Ownership of risk

In contrast to most so-called partnership deals, risk is not shared between client and contractors. BAA carries it all, allowing contractors to concentrate on delivering results. The focus is on managing out the cause of problems, not their effects if they do happen.

Complexity management

The task of building T5 is split into 16 main projects, plus 147 sub-projects of between £30 million and £150 million each. The agreement binds BAA and its 60 key first-tier' suppliers only, these suppliers are themselves responsible for the appointment and management of second- and third-tier suppliers, who must also work within the spirit of the agreement.

Close supplier involvement

To avoid the traditional and potentially damaging demarcation between design and build, key suppliers were brought on board at a much earlier stage in the planning process than is usual. This enabled potential hitches to be spotted before designs were finalised and construction began.

Integrated teamwork
Both within and across teams, the concentration has been on proactive problem-solving rather than the avoidance of litigation.

Shared values
Common induction programmes and regular communication initiatives help to ensure that all of the 6,000 workers from 400 supplier companies who can be involved at any given time share the same values and objectives, which include being proud of working on T5 and delivering the project on time, on budget, to quality and safely. – *Human Resources*, November 2004.

2005: Contracting: Adversary or Collaboration?
The £757 million Wembley National Stadium is one of the largest, most costly and complex construction schemes in the UK. Like all mega-projects, it poses enormous technical and logistical challenges. How a project is procured has a huge bearing on whether problems arise, and whether disputes break out between different parts of the construction team.

The stadium, which is scheduled to open on 13 May 2006, is being built under a design-and-build contract. This is a modern procurement method under which the main contractor (Multiplex at Wembley) in effect becomes the agent for the client, as well as being responsible for building the job.

This is a departure from the norm as traditionally; clients would deal independently with a designer, quantity surveyor and main contractor. Under design-and-build, however, the main contractor becomes the client's single point of contact, managing all other contractual relationships and the associated construction risks. The contract was also let on a fixed-price, lump-sum basis, shifting project risk to the contractor.

Dumping risk

Simon Murray, chairman of contractor Geoffrey Osborne and former director of major projects at Railtrack, says that in principle, "having a single party who you deal with and who takes responsibility is good, but it shouldn't be absolute. It's naive to put all risk onto the team doing the project. And if you are doing something of national significance, the idea that you can dump risk is absurd."

Risk dumping happens when companies pass responsibility for danger or problems that may occur during construction to firms they hire to do work for them.

"Main contractors' relationships with the supply chain are very patchy," Murray says. "There are some who want to get the lowest possible price and dump risk on the people they hire to do the work. Yet those who really know how to do things are the suppliers and specialist contractors."

He contends that lowest price generally offers a false economy, since it forces suppliers to compromise on the quality of their technical solution.

Graham Edgell, group procurement director at contractor Morgan Sindall, agrees: "A lot of clients are after a quick process — they just want the job done, without any added-value. Because we make such a stupendous effort for such small reward, and our guys are under such pressure to deliver for the sum agreed, there's no opportunity of letting your guard down. You've tied yourself to a price and then you've got to go out and do it."

Despite the UK construction industry tradition of firms "buying work" — taking on projects at cost, simply to keep its people and plant active — British firms walked away from Wembley. Multiplex, however, claimed it could deliver the job for the price offered, and told its shareholders it would turn in a profit.

Adversary relationships

Wembley's great technical challenge was the structural design, construction and erection of its signature arch. Multiplex awarded steelwork firm Cleveland Bridge a lump-sum, fixed-price subcontract to fabricate, supply, deliver and erect the arch and roof. However, this deal has encountered problems. In a claim against Multiplex for non-payment, Cleveland Bridge alleges that "by spring of 2003 there were serious problems arising from late and incomplete design by the civil and structural engineer, and delays in providing design information. The design changes and late information caused substantial costs increases, and delays and disruption to the subcontract works." Though Cleveland Bridge and Multiplex agreed a plan for accelerating work, plus compensation for the resulting change in the subcontract terms, a legal row then broke out, over alleged non-payment and contract breaches.

Despite the integration that should have been achieved by using a design-and-build contract, "Wembley is a graphic example of old-style adversarial contracting," according to Bob White, chief executive of Constructing Excellence, who have the task of improving performance in the construction industry.

Despite the problems construction consultant Frank Griffiths says, "Wembley thought that a fixed-price, lump-sum contract could be the solution to all its problems. But that is only fine if the contractor has all the resources, time and money required for the project." For such a contract to work, he adds, there has to be a rigorous work programme in place, and the client also needs to understand how the work is going to be subcontracted. "Through using a design and build contract, Wembley thought it had offloaded risk to Multiplex, but it hadn't."

BAA and Collaborative approach
Other such mega-projects have taken a different approach. British Airports Authority (BAA), which is building Heathrow's Terminal 5 and they have enormous in-house procurement and project management teams, which supervise and reduce risk at all stages of design and construction.

"BAA has spent a fortune on ensuring they're informed," says Gil Howarth, founder of project management company Howarth Associates. Both have elected to work in partnership with their contractors, using the same offices, sharing information and resources, and, crucially, any savings or overruns.

BAA ditched conventional, reactive contracts, in which one party claims against another for delays or extra costs, in favour of creating incentives for proactive behaviour that would pre-empt problems. This tactic was guided by study of other major construction schemes, which revealed that, as a client, pushing risk to arm's length offered no real protection. "The client is always accountable in the end, on cost, time and health and safety — everything," says Riley. If the project were to go wrong, its failings would have an impact on BAA's reputation in the industry and on its standing in the City."

BAA took the radical step of accepting all risk, and took out £4 billion worth of insurance. "By doing that you take away negativity, allow space for innovation and create the opportunity for people to perform at levels they haven't been allowed to before," explains Riley.

A special contract, the Terminal 5 Agreement, was produced for the project, requiring totally integrated teams, including principal subcontractors up through main contractors and designers to BAA itself and British Airways, Terminal S's end user. Contractors are paid on a cost- reimbursable basis, with performance encouraged by offering bonuses for beating target costs and completion dates; conversely, they share some of BAA's "pain" when schedules and costs overran.

The agreement engaged all the key players early on to identify risks well before they come into the construction programme, leading to highly evolved risk-management strategies.

Cost efficiencies

The style of collaborative project management practised by BAA grew out of the North Sea oil and gas industry 30 years ago, and was being adapted for the construction sector by BAA and other clients more than a decade ago. But partnering only grabbed attention following the publication of two government-sponsored reports in 1994 and 1998 respectively, *Constructing the Team*, authored by Sir Michael Latham, and *Rethinking Construction*, by Sir John Egan.

Egan calculated the UK's £58-billion a year construction sector could achieve cost efficiencies of 30 per cent, reduce defects by 20 per cent and increase profitability from 2 per cent to 5 per cent by developing better leadership and greater focus on customer needs, by integrating processes and teams, and by adopting an agenda driven by quality rather than cost.

For clients, this meant releasing large volumes of work in a steady stream to give contractors more continuity, and adopting them as preferred suppliers. For contractors, it meant breaking the practice of paying subcontractors late and of casually hiring and firing labour.

Egan urged: "Industry must replace competitive tendering with long-term relationships based on clear measurement of performance and sustained improvements in quality and efficiency."
– Extracts from "A Game of Two Halves" in *Supply Management,* 6 October 2005, by Andrew Mylius (the features editor of *New Civil Engineer*).

The above examples represent some of the recent UK history in introducing relationships into the supply chain. We will continue by looking at some more specific examples.

Appendix 2: Case Studies on Collaboration

Case Study | The essential ingredients of successful partnerships

The essential ingredients of successful partnership include:
- Genuine commitment from the top of both organisations.
- A firm understanding by both parties of what is expected - in generalities and specifics.
- Capable people sufficiently trained to carry out the job.
- Sufficient resources to ensure success.
- Patience to tackle obstacles and teething problems.
- Open communication; and action as well as words.

- Most of all, however, partnership demands trust.

"Trust is the most important word in the whole business," says one materials manager, "and one of the most difficult tasks is to convince people there is real meaning behind that word."

Negative attitudes built up over years will take time to change. Buyers and suppliers have traditionally been antagonists in the fight to secure a competitive advantage; now they are being asked to bury the hatchet and become colleagues. How well they succeed will depend largely on how well they have understood the concept; as well as providing an indication of the calibre of the personnel. But once the philosophy has been taken on board, it will help unleash productivity and creative potential in your company which has lying dormant.

Good communication is almost as vital as trust. "The problem with British industry" complained the head of one Scottish sub-contracting firm "is that not enough time is spent talking with people."

In partnerships, people are continually talking about needs, expectations, problems and ideas; both inside their own company and with their partners.

Newcomers to partnership approaches, need patience to overcome teething problems. As in any relationship, flexibility is also important. When a fault develops in a traditional trading arrangement, the first reaction is to apportion blame. In partnerships things are done differently: the partners look for what's wrong and put it right.

Partnerships involve the exchange of information which, before, might have been available only to a few senior managers in their own companies. In some instances, open-book costing (where the customer has access to the supplier's accounts for cost reduction projects) is used. This is a perfect illustration of where complete trust is needed. Agreements requiring that confidences be kept can (and should) be drawn up, but no contract can replace genuine trust.

Case Study

Telecoms: SRM according to Orange

"My vision was simple," says Allison Ford-Langstaff, director of sourcing and SRM at Orange. "I wanted to create a programme that demonstrated and communicated our understanding of our supply base. And I wanted it to show, through tangible business KPIs, how buyers working alongside internal stakeholders bring about value."

In late 2008, Ford-Langstaff took on responsibility for SRM agenda at the telecommunications firm. Previously, Orange had managed many of its individual relationships well but there was no consistency across categories and no overall strategy. Here's what they did, and how.

Four steps to success

Orange designed what it called the `SRM pathway', setting out four steps it needed to take:

* segmenting the supply base
* supplier performance measurement
* strategic relationship management
* continuous improvement

It wanted buyers to have complete responsibility for the sourcing process, so it created a small team dedicated to SRM to move things forward. In February 2009 Rachel Scarrett, who was formally head of category for marketing sourcing at Orange, was appointed head of SRM. Having a sourcing professional lead this new team was a deliberate move to ensure SRM had a genuine practical application and "did not remain darkened room theory", says Ford-Langstaff.

Although many academic studies had been conducted on SRM, the team found that few organisations had turned theory into practice with tangible benefits.

1. Segmentation

The first major undertaking was to ensure the supply base was segmented so Orange could allocate resources to deliver the most value. This was already done to a certain extent but was predominantly based on it's spend profile. The SRM team developed a tool for buyers to review suppliers which took into account other factors, such as business risk and opportunity. Stakeholders were also included.

The company now reviews its segmentation annually, with a checkpoint every six months to ensure market alterations are accounted for.

2. Supplier performance measurement

Next, it had to find a way to measure supplier performance: a journey Orange describes as "fairly painful". It developed a scorecard covering quality, responsiveness, environment, delivery, innovation and cost, but underestimated how difficult it would be to get such a large group of buyers to alter the way they measured performance.

Previously, each sourcing team had its own means of measurement based on what best suited that particular supply base and stakeholders, but through "stealth and an unbending belief", Orange says, it managed to phase in its standard performance measurement programme starting with marketing and professional services, customer equipment, then networks and IT. This staggered approach meant the process could be tweaked as issues arose.

The initial training was a great start but buyers needed ongoing support from managers and the SRM team to set targets, calculate the results and draw enough insight from the scorecards to set meaningful action plans for continuous improvement. In late 2009, the scorecard became an in-house built online tool called 'iScore'. This allows buyers, stakeholders and suppliers to set, record and report performance data direct in to the system as well as provide action plans and other useful intelligence.

3. Strategic relationship management

Orange says it already had excellent internal relationships with business stakeholders but there was still room to act in a more joined up way when managing suppliers.

Using the new segmentation as a base, the team created a method which set out the type and frequency of meetings held and the appropriate level of performance measurement. This governance applies to anyone working in the company who works with a supplier, even the executive team. Having one view of a supplier enables it to manage the relationship better and feedback from vendors has been very positive.

4. Continuous improvement

Ford-Langstaff admits this step is still in its infancy but at its heart is ensuring buyers are equipped with sophisticated tools and techniques to carve out long-term value.

Orange launched in-house training for buyers in late 2008, with the focus on getting the basics in place. In addition, the company aims to pilot a small number of joint initiatives with selected suppliers with the objective of creating value. This could be through elimination of waste, joint development projects, shared intelligence or early access to innovation.

Ford-Langstaff says Orange's sourcing organisation and its suppliers are both a strategic asset. It provides a learning opportunity for people in sourcing and the chance to shout about suppliers who have made an outstanding contribution to the company.

Communication

The right communications plan was essential to allow the SRM transformation to take place. In addition to training, guidelines, meetings and workshops, a team of SRM champions was created to put in place consistent best practice across the business.

"This was to ensure the SRM team did not become another ivory tower, full of theory but easily ignored by the buying teams," says Ford-Langstaff.

A representative from each of the major sourcing categories was chosen to work with Scarrett as part of their buying role. Not only do they ensure new initiatives are fit for purpose, they also use their influence with peers to sell the benefits, and provide knowledge and training.

Scarrett adds: "The concept of an SRM champion is simple but the benefits have been significant. It would be easy to make incorrect assumptions about how categories operate. The champions work with me to ensure we have a fully informed debate. Likewise, buying teams have a spokesperson."

Like many sourcing functions, Orange measures savings performance but the SRM programme now gives facts on supplier performance and the financial contribution SRM makes. This is reported quarterly to the executive team and means sourcing can demonstrate what SRM delivers, so far, incremental savings of 23%.

– *Supply Management*, 18 March 2010

Case Study

Construction and Wolseley Supply Chain

The UK Construction Industry

Construction is one of the UK's largest industries, contributing 10% to the UK's GDP, its output is three times that of agriculture and larger than any single manufacturing industry It also has the largest workforce, employing more than two million people.

However, despite the significant advances in design, product and process innovation by a vanguard of enlightened companies, the majority of the UK construction industry, particularly at grass roots level, retains many inefficient and outdated practices, which have long since disappeared other industry sectors. One of the biggest challenges facing the sector, at a time when skilled labour is increasingly rare and expensive, is the need to ensure that when labour is available it is used productively to increase project efficiency. That means getting materials to the right place at the right time.

The report of the "Rethinking Construction" Task Force, published in July 1998, highlighted logistics and supply chain management as one of many areas where the UK construction industry could improve, particularly by taking note of and learning from, the ways in which other industry sectors operate. The report cited 'lean' processes, as used in the car industry as a vital means of obtaining sustained improvements in performance a bringing the construction sector up to standards being achieved in many other of industry

Six years on, there is still much work to inefficiency and waste remains barriers to improved performance for many in the construction supply chain.

Wolseley

Wolseley UK, one of the largest distribution companies of construction, heating and plumbing materials, is one of the enlightened companies within construction which has seen that sophisticated logistics practices and robust supply chain management are essential to achieving sustainable improvement.

Garry Flanagan is director of logistics at Wolseley UK. He sees the company's role as being the 'lynchpin' in the supply chain, which brings materials from the manufacturers to the sites where they are needed. "The use of a sophisticated logistics system can ensure that materials are delivered on site at exactly the right time. In the most successful cases, a carefully managed merchant-contractor relationship can make it possible to deliver to 30-minute windows into brown field construction sites in urban areas. The closer relationship merchants have with contractors and sub-contractors and their logistics and supply chain systems mean that they can provide the right supply solution for each client.

Efficiency gains

Wolseley UK has also used its extensive distribution network to take cost out of the extended supply chain (the combined Supplier-Wolseley UK supply chain). This is done by integrating suppliers' and Wolseley UK's supply lines to share the benefit of the resulting efficiency gains.

Flanagan continues: "Our national network of distribution centre and branches enables us to provide an unrivalled delivery promise and nationwide access to our products and services. We provide our customers with a variety of added-value services, and ensure a tailored approach to their needs including direct delivery from our distribution centres and off-site prefabrication. The Wolseley UK trade park initiatives and express high street branches also offer customers even greater accessibility to our products and a higher level of convenience."

Partnership and reduced costs

Wolseley UK and Taylor Woodrow are piloting a partnership scheme on a housing development at Breme Park, Bromsgrove. The 104-dwelling development is a mixture of three-storey apartments as well as two, three and four bedroom houses. It is the first time a partnership of this kind has been undertaken with a house builder. The company has a mini- branch on site manned full-time by Andy King, a Wolseley UK employee with more than 20 years' experience in the construction industry. Through close liaison with the site manager and links to both Wolseley UK and Taylor Woodrow's IT systems on-site, King manages all of the ordering and delivery of materials on Taylor Woodrow's behalf.

King's understanding of the build process, combined with knowing exactly which stage of construction each unit has reached, radically improves efficiency. The only materials brought on site are those that are needed. Wolseley's bulk distribution sites at Dudley and Northampton package the materials for each specific unit and they are either delivered direct to the plot or held in an on-site compound ready for delivery the following day. Smaller items are assembled into plot lots on site.

The main challenge that Wolseley and Taylor Woodrow have faced is the resistance to change, which is ingrained in the culture of the industry. This resistance means it can take a lot of effort and a long time to make progress, reach agreement and establish terms and conditions.

However, having seen the partnership in action this resistance is melting away, but it has taken absolute proof of the benefits to convince people that the old method of procurement was not necessarily the best. With materials taken care of, the site manager is free to concentrate on the build programme. Having more time to spend working with sub-contractors means problems can be identified and overcome quickly which leads to improved quality and less snagging at the end of the build phase, which reduces costs and avoids tying up skilled labour for longer than is absolutely necessary. Before the pilot, the site manager spent 60% of his time chasing materials and managing deliveries. This has been reduced by 50% and when the pilot moves to phase two, where all subcontractors also buy through Wolseley UK this will reduce further.

The project is currently ahead of schedule and in the interests of continuous improvement, Wolseley and Taylor Woodrow are working to establish and measure the financial savings, time savings and the increase in productivity that have resulted from this collaboration.

It is clear that Wolseley UK is making great strides in improving efficiency and leading the way in developing supply chain solutions to meet customers' needs. In the industry at large, however a significant step change is still required to bring logistics and supply chain management up to the standards of many other commercial and industrial sectors. Flanagan comments: "The only way that the industry can make any real progress is by developing close partnerships between suppliers and customers and for supply chain integration to become part of the culture of construction. He continues: "Our team of supply chain professionals will focus on taking our supply chain to the next stage of development across warehousing, transport, demand and supply planning. We also have a supply chain development team, which will design and implement the strategy for Wolseley UK over the coming years. We are also focused on sharing best practice across the Wolseley group and beyond through a supply chain committee and we aim to achieve a results-based culture through key performance indicators and rewarding individuals and teams on the basis of their performance."

Through working with its supply base and customers, Wolseley UK will continue to take advantage of integration and collaboration opportunities to drive down cost and offer unrivalled service. Flanagan concludes: "Collaboration and supply chain integration is the key to the successful future of construction logistics. Partnership with our suppliers enables us to share demand data to improve product availability and successfully bring new products to market. Partnership with our customers allows us to better understand their needs and provide a tailored end-to-end solution to their needs."

– extracts from: *Logistics Manager,* March 2005

Case Study | A UK Car Assembler's Supply strategy

The company has a focused product supply strategy that is integrally linked to the philosophy of the 'extended enterprise' where the destinies of suppliers, dealers and workers at every level of the business are inseparable. This is reinforced through promotional and marketing messages which stress the responsibility the company owes to its dealer network. The former chairman had previously and publicly threw down the gauntlet to component suppliers, in a bid to make them understand that the company was not a meal ticket. Nowadays, threats are replaced by promises. The following statement for the MD explains their current position:

"Our relationship with the supply community today is very pervasive. It is not just about price and output any more, nor has it been for a long time; but it is about culture, management style and about whether the right things are happening within the framework of the business for a particular partner to be someone in whom we can invest a long term, life time partnership relationship. You have to handle it with care."

The company now recognizes that a supplier can be a positive partner and a loyal companion while serving different customers, and that having different dialogues can be healthy.

"We have to share the benefits, to understand that you cannot have a lifetime relationship unless the partner is financially healthy, but that achieving this does not introduce a price and cost structure that is uncompetitive to the end product," the MD says. "At one time, people would say, 'if we do this, it will benefit X, Y and Z as well, but we take the view that you waste a lot of time in that narrow mind-set.

It is more productive to think about the fact that by both of you being involved there is a benefit of shared knowledge and experience which benefits everyone, in particular your customers. We have recognized that just because you happen to be the biggest link in the chain which comprises the extended enterprise, this does not imply superiority. You need to use your facilities, resources and even your philosophical capability to extend processes in all directions, both internally and externally."

The retail sector was very active with collaboration, on an individual company basis, in the 1990's. Some organisations though were slow starters, indeed a comment made to the author by a major UK retail company in the early 1990's was that "partnershaft" was preferred over the word partnership; this reflecting their current adversarial methods.

Case Study

Food Retail (Iceland and supplier collaboration)

Iceland, part of the Big Food Group, is a high street supermarket chain with 760 stores across the UK and Ireland. In Iceland's 2003 annual report, it set out two strategic objectives — to develop organisation processes and people that enable efficiency and innovation; and build a reputation with suppliers as the most constructive and innovative channel to market. To achieve that, the company would have to move away from a co-managed inventory and adopt a collaborative supply chain.

Also, Iceland felt that creating a closer working relationship with suppliers would lead to efficiencies and eliminate waste within its supply chain. As such, it is one of the first retailers in Europe to allow suppliers to have visibility from the factory through to the store.

Sharing information with suppliers has dramatically increased event and promotion effectiveness, reduced distribution costs and decreased warehouse stock. Ultimately, Iceland is closer to its customers in offering the products that they want.

As a result, Iceland launched a unique collaborative initiative with many of its key suppliers. Overall, the initiative has strengthened supplier partnerships while managing the extended supply chain proactively and eliminating waste. Before this initiative, a supplier to Iceland was essentially working with limited information in an uncertain environment, resulting in markdowns or inefficient use of transport. Few suppliers had visibility beyond their despatches or knowledge of the Iceland business.

When information was shared, suppliers could not react quickly enough to changes in stock requirements and increased consumer demand.

James Hulse, Iceland's supplier development manager, comments: "Suppliers rarely have sight of their products once they leave their factories, so we needed to give them a line of sight into the business. Getting forecasts wrong can and does lead to significant cases of overstock. By allowing our suppliers to get more involved in the entire supply chain, we knew we could benefit from few stock-outs, improved availability, more successful promotions and, ultimately, better customer service."

Product management
Using Portfolio Allocation and Replenishment solutions from JDA Software and innovative business practices, a number of Iceland's suppliers can now tap directly into the company's

store level replenishment data to improve on-demand forecasts.

After running a successful pilot and training in 2003, Iceland and its chosen suppliers have accumulated a wide array of benefits. Because residual stocks, packaging and raw materials cannot necessarily be used for other products, greater supply chain visibility has been particularly beneficial for the suppliers of Iceland's own-label products, including Sun Valley Foods. Hulse says: "We are now giving our suppliers access to the store as well as warehouse data required to help them manage their business with us more effectively."

Since the introduction of the initiative, Sun Valley Foods also observed significantly lower distribution costs and increased vehicle use. This year it has achieved the lowest average pallet rate ever with Iceland. The company also boosted its confidence to improve manufacturing efficiency. Sun Valley Foods' supply chain planning manager, Ian Parkes, explains: "We try to deliver into Iceland less frequently with fuller loads, so we've reduced delivery costs significantly, partly by sharing loads with another supplier." Demand for fresh produce can now be forecasted more accurately. According to Hulse, in certain cases this has resulted in the elimination of warehouse stock that has created an additional one to two days of shelf life in store — meaning fresher produce for the consumer. Other benefits include:

- Improved service levels.
- Faster flow of product through the supply chain.
- Rational use of resources and more effective promotion planning.
- Synchronisation of production to better match supply with demand.
- Shared responsibility and mutual trust.

Building on the success of its early partners (Coca-Cola, Deans Foods, Rye Valley, Schwans and Sun Valley), Iceland's program has been progressively rolled out since June 2003 with other targeted suppliers. At least 18 suppliers are now up and running. Hulse says: "The payback has been quick which has made the investment required definitely worth it. Every supplier tells us that trading relationships have improved dramatically. And it's not just the financial return, it's also the soft benefits that everyone is talking about, such as being able to plan promotions more effectively and working more efficiently together."

– extracts from *Logistics Manager*, June 2004

Case Study

FMCG Production (Proctor & Gamble)

US owned group Procter & Gamble (P&G) manufactures and markets nearly 300 brands of consumer products including household names Lenor, Ariel, Pampers, Sunny Delight and Pringles. With a workforce of nearly 100,000 worldwide, the group operates in nearly 80 countries worldwide and made net sales of almost US$43.4Bn (£24.5Bn) in the 12 months to June 2003. However while the organisation was built up into the "fantastically good" manufacturing organisation that it is today, its supply chain was inefficient.

As a result the company has been transforming its UK supply chain into an efficient and collaborative operation. This process has involved implementing a range of innovative schemes to help optimise and consolidate the supply chain and the group's "first time fill rate" for customers now stands at 90%.

The transformation has proved so successful that the trailblazing ideas are now being introduced elsewhere within P&G's European supply chain.

The challenge of revolutionising the group's UK supply chain has been the responsibility of Chris Poole P&G's logistics director for the UK and Ireland and co-chair of consumer industry body ECR UK. The group's new philosophy, explains Poole, is all about "winning at the first moment of truth. It is important that we make sure product is there at the store, looks good on the shelf, and has been delivered in the most cost-efficient way so that those cost savings can be ultimately incorporated into a lower cost. That's not new. It's just about great service and low costs, and trying to get that balance".

The transformation of P&G's UK supply chain began after three areas were identified that had to be dealt with in order to deliver a great on-shelf service. Poole explains: "The first is that we have to deliver a great basic service, we have to be good at the fundamentals. We don't have the licence to do anything else with customers unless we are fantastic at that. Secondly, we have to and want to collaborate very closely with customers. We can't do it by ourselves. And thirdly, we must work now on the future. We have to be innovative."

Poole continues: "The great basic service is about delivering what customers want, damage-free and on time, and we weren't very good at these five years ago". "We invested over US$40M to upgrade our whole logistics infrastructure."

The changes included:
- Focusing on supplier relationship management and improving the speed and accuracy of information flow up the supply chain,
- Creating two distribution centres in the North and

South to deliver the full range of P&G's ambient products on one truck.

- Introducing innovative schemes such as cross-docking so that products bypass storage, saving time and resources by going straight onto store shelves.
- Using IT solutions such as GPS tracking and electronic proof of delivery.

P&G has also introduced joint forecasting within its supply chain. Poole explains: "Joint forecasting is about sitting down and agreeing quantities and delivery times together so that there are no surprises. With each of our customers we set up joint forecasting processes and for big customers and big promotions the forecasting detail – when they need it, how much is needed and delivery time – has to be signed off by the logistics and the commercial people on both sides, so that everybody knows what the deal is. The nightmares only come because there are surprises through lack of communication."

Working with customers has improved P&G's service levels but, says Poole, the crusade continues. "Collaboration with customers is critical. You have to get in with the customers and understand what they want, working through the solution. Anything that improves service on shelf and reduces total supply chain costs from the factory gate outwards is up for grabs.

"What we don't want is to shunt value around the supply chain, we used to do that when customers had three sources to deal with — we were saying 'to get the best price you've got to order a truckload' and they would do that. What we were actually doing was washing our hands of it, and that wasn't good enough. All we did there was shunt the inventory and the problem onto another supply chain."

Poole stresses that companies have to sit down with customers and create a "logistics hit-list" highlighting the areas that will be mutually beneficial, improve service and reduce total supply chain costs. "That's the basis of our collaboration with any customer — let's work together to find the best way to improve service and reduce costs."

In transforming its supply chain, P&G also approached major customers for input on improving its supply chain. "That's not to say we did everything they said," says Poole, "but we listened to them. And that's how it continues now. The collaboration work is based on what we can do to improve the flow of information up the supply chain; how we can make that faster and more accurate."

Poole believes collaboration with customers is key to an efficient supply chain. He concludes: "A real focus on joint and collaborative planning with customers has been critical. It's all very well putting in great capability and structurally changing our supply chain but at the end of the day you can't make it happen unless you work with your customer."

– extracts from *Logistics Manager*, June 2004

Case Study

3PL and Collaboration

Faced with the dual challenge of taking £20 million-worth of inventory out of its supply chain and driving productivity improvements across its distribution network, DIY retailer Homebase has leveraged its collaborative relationship with Unipart Logistics to deliver on its objectives.

Homebase is one of the UK's most readily recognised retail

brands. As the second largest home improvement retailer in the country, the company sells over 30,000 products across its DIY and decorating and home and garden ranges, and has a growing internet offering. Homebase serves over 70 million customers a year through its network of around 350 large, out-of-town stores and has plans in place to add 15 new stores a year.

Maintaining on-shelf availability across its retail network with such a diverse product range is a daily challenge for Nigel Basey, Head of Distribution, Homebase. Against this daily requirement for high product availability, he has been working to achieve the company's ambitious goal on inventory, Homebase has been engaged for the past two years in a strategic pain to reduce inventory by £20 million a year in order to improve cash flow.

Working closely with logistics service partner Unipart Logistics, Homebase has made significant reductions to stock holdings, improved productivity within the supply chain, cut costs and radically restructured its distribution centre network to bring the financial benefits sought. At the same time, it has improved on-shelf availability. Nigel Basey describes the implications of the reduced stock holding on the company's distribution network: "We now need less warehouse space and because Unipart Logistics has been flexible in being able to accommodate additional ranges from other DCs, we have been able to rationalise our network infrastructure"'

The success of the relationship between retailer and logistics service provider has seen Unipart Logistics' role grow substantially over the last five years, to a point where it is now responsible for between 30 and 40% of the volume of goods going to Homebase stores.

Nigel Basey describes how 'Project Bentley', the transfer of the pots and tiles ranges to the Cowley facility, has benefited the company: "Absorbing those ranges into the Cowley operation demonstrated great flexibility, without any major increases in space and cost. Productivity and efficiency of the operation was maintained throughout, and TUPE transfer was effected extremely smoothly and competently But importantly, the service to stores was seamless, which was a big risk factor when we entered into the project.'

Along with the large cost savings and efficiency gains from rationalising the network, Homebase has also benefited from Unipart Logistics' analytical approach to tackling issues around product shrinkage in the pots and tiles supply chain, Shrinkage and damage were costly problems for Homebase. Andy Pearce, Account Manager for the Homebase contract at Unipart Logistics, explains: "We looked at how the product was being brought in from Turkey and the Far East and worked with a cross-functional team at Homebase to understand where the losses were occurring and made interventions to address the issues including the development of better packaging solutions from factory to store. We also paid close attention to the way the product was handled at the DC and in store. Due to this collaborative approach, Homebase has seen a 30% reduction in shrinkage on those products."

Giving an indication as to the scale of the ramping up of operations for Homebase, Andy Pearce says, "When we first started, we had 400 SKUs and had a weekly throughput of about 60,000 cases: that's 30,000 in, 30,000 out. Now a normal week is 300,000 cases in, 300,000 out, and we will pick 60,000 cases a day. So we are doing double in a day what we were doing for a whole week five years ago." The number of SKUs has increased dramatically, too, rising to the present level of 2500: "a large proportion of the products we handle have the greatest range change for Homebase. So we have to manage the change very carefully, clearing the old stock through and ensuring that the new stock is in every store and ready to go when Homebase announces a new range".

One of the most striking aspects of the Cowley NIC is that it is a conventional warehouse operation, in that it is not reliant on automation; but it is unconventional, perhaps, in terms of the lean practices by which it is run. Employee engagement and individual development are core aspects of Unipart Logistics management principles. These are set in motion by a stepped approach to developing staff known as the "Gate to Great" journey that leads the individual through five levels of role development; see, learn, do, teach, coach.

The Unipart Way encourages staff to work in teams and constantly to monitor and question the efficiency of the tasks they perform. Teams meet on a daily, weekly and monthly basis to review performance against key performance indicators and a series of tools are used to examine processes in order to drive performance, delivering greater value to the customer.

Visual management techniques are also used to enhance operational performance by speeding decision-making and cutting errors, and display boards are deployed to provide feedback to staff on their performance. Mapping processes, creating- work sequences and determining information flows for a particular task are all part of the Unipart Way and are used to remove waste from each process.

Ensuring that an operation the size of the Cowley NIC runs to the greatest efficiency requires the constant measurement of performance. Over 30 KPIs are used to monitor such activities as receiving goods, putting them away, through picking, packing and despatch. Each process is accounted for in terms of quality, accuracy and time. Andy Pearce explains that pick accuracy is critical: "As stores do not check deliveries on receipt, simply the containers, pick accuracy is extremely important. At present we operate to 99.7%. However; there is an opportunity to take this further by working with suppliers to incorporate bar codes at source".

Beyond the warehouse environment, Unipart Logics has been working with Homebase on using the Unipart Way to help retail stores improve efficiencies from receipt of goods through to the-shelf. Now the retailer is looking at the opportunities that exist in leveraging Unipart Logistics' facilities in the Far East for consolidating in-bound goods from a number of sources which will allow greater flexibility and a reduction in inventory costs.

Further projects are also in progress. Plans are underway to invest in the layout of facilities at Cowley to improve productivity by an additional 10%, increasing internal storage by 18% on the same footprint.

These projects are just part of the ongoing collaboration between the service prouder and the retailer, actions that are delivering a constant stream of productivity improvements and cost reductions making a true working partnership that achieves mutual benefit.

"We operate a true partnership with Unipart Logistics and there is a great level of understanding between the two businesses. Both are committed to continuous improvement cost reduction and a lean approach," says Nigel Basey. "There has been a tremendous amount of flexibly from the Unipart team and they have never turned down volume. What's more, they have always done what they said they would do, they

have always honoured their commitments, and that's why we have a high degree of trust and confidence in them".
– By Nick Allen, extracts from *Focus*, Volume 13 number 6 June 2011: ciltuk.org

Case Study | Royal Mint: Keeping in contact

Phil Carpenter, executive director of operations, The Royal Mint, explains how drive, focus and taking time to talk to people are key when it comes to developing good relationships.

'I am responsible for all manufacturing, engineering, maintenance, planning and operational excellence at The Royal Mint. The relationship we have with procurement is very good and adds a huge amount of value to the business overall. It's in line with The Royal Mint's strategy of working as one team - working for what we call 'the country' (the whole organisation) rather than just the club' (an individual department).

Things between procurement and operations changed when Gail Roberts, director of supply chain, joined The Royal Mint in 2009. You need to have people at senior level who is committed to making it work and who can get some momentum. If they have drive and focus and are consistent, people pick up on that and follow their lead. For that to happen, you need to ensure you demonstrate a set of values and are clear about what needs to be done. If you don't have interpersonal relationships at all levels you lose the ability to challenge and if you lose that, you stop moving forward.

There are an increasing number of examples where our

closer ties have brought about business improvements. One example is our links with a supplier of mild steel coil.

Better links between the technical team, the supplier and the commercial department meant we got improvements in terms of flexibility on lead times and deliveries, while the supplier benefited from understanding our future volume and quality requirements.

Operations people often ask for what they think they want, not what they actually need, so challenging specifications can help. Equally, if the operations team has close links with a supplier, it can help commercial colleagues understand what can be expected, which helps negotiations.

To develop good relationships with your stakeholders or internal customers, face-to-face contact is key. You don't get that level of understanding if you don't take the time to talk to people and see what they do – and they appreciate you making the effort, which strengthens the relationship.

While things have vastly improved here, we do recognise we need to develop it further. For example, operations are better at persuading engineers that they're not necessarily the best people to do commercial contracts and deal with suppliers. It's got better, but it doesn't happen all the time.'

How it works at the royal mint
The Royal Mint's procurement and operations teams have forged closer links with a clear set of values that the teams can follow, in line with the organisation's strategy of working as one team.

1. Get out and meet your internal customers face-to-face. I've yet to see an example where a relationship is developed better by email.

2. Be consistent – your actions and your attitude will then be copied by others.

4. You have to be honest and open with each other to challenge each other to progress things for the good of the business.

5. Aim for the outcome to benefit the organisation as a whole, not just your department.

6. Keep it up. It's not easy, it doesn't happen by accident you have to work at it like any relationship, but if you're consistent in your approach it will deliver benefits.

– *Supply Management*, 1 January 2012

Case Study

Making an end-to-end Supply Chain Green

The GFTN/WWF initiative full case study is in *Green Supply Chains – an action manifesto*, by Emmett and Sood: 2010. Selected extracts are shown here.

The Supply Chain, whilst is an embracive and total concept, is really a philosophical approach. This means therefore that any supply chain approach on for example, creating a green supply chain, can mean different things to different people.

The term "Supply Chain" primarily covers:

- Everything between Supply and Demand;
- The movement of materials/inventory/information;
- From Suppliers to Company to Customers; and doing this in a Timely manner to meet the customers demand requirements.

There is usually going to be more than one supply chain in any one organisation and the supply chain processes and activities will represent between 30 to 70% of the organisations business cost.

The Supply chain will also reach locally, regionally and globally; meanwhile, every supply chain will be driven by demand, as if there is no demand, then there is no supply.

Every product supply chain will ultimately involve every one of the following standard economic sectors.

Primary sector: Raw materials from farming/fishing (food, beverages, and forestry), quarrying/mining (minerals, coals, metals) or drilling (oil, gas, water).

Secondary sector: Conversion of these raw materials into products by milling, smelting, extracting, refining into oils/chemicals/products and then maybe; machining, fabricating, moulding, assembly, mixing, processing, constructing into components, sub assemblies, building construction/structures and furniture/electronic/food/paper/metal/chemicals and plastic products.

Service or tertiary sector: business, personal and entertainment services, which involve the channels of distribution from suppliers to customers, via direct, wholesale or retail channels. Services include packaging, physical distribution, hotels, catering, banking, insurance, finance, education, public sector, post, telecoms, retail, repairs etc.

These sectors are all located globally, as no one country has a single total ownership of every one of these sectors, indeed, as popularized by the former US President, Ronald Reagan, "we live in a global village" (this term was actually coined in 1962 by Canadian media theorist Marshall McLuhan).

The Supply Chain philosophy and approach therefore aims

to integrate, locally to globally, all of the flows of information, physical goods and product/services flows, the money flows and any returning or recycling or reverse flows.

The Supply Chain can be labelled as involving all of the "ground to ground" flow processes, where the successful integration, will provide a competitive edge in the marketplace, for those organisations who apply the philosophy. In so doing, SCM will add value and remove waste. The use of word "ground" representing the literal origin and source of raw materials and also, the eventual return to the ground of the ultimate and final product disposal to landfill (which is directly a Green issue).

Managing the Supply Chain however does not actually start with Supply as the Supply Chain is always triggered and started by Demand; it is ultimately the end consumer demand that drives everything. This end demand being then adjusted and changed and passed on through all of the appropriate supply sides of the services and secondary sectors to the other end; the supply from the primary sector.

There are very few examples of the management of the "end to end" or "start to finish" supply chains that will take such a total global managed view from the initial triggering end of the consumer demand, right through to the other end of the primary sector supply; one reason for such few examples is that to do this and do it on a global basis, is an enormous challenge.

Such a challenge has however been successfully taken on by the Global Forest & Trade Network (GFTN); an initiative of the global conservation organisation WWF to eliminate the supply of illegal wood and transform the global demand marketplace, for timber and paper products, into a force for saving the world's valuable and threatened forests.

The GFTN does this by facilitating trade links between companies that are committed to achieving and supporting responsible forestry. The GFTN then creates market conditions that do help to conserve the world's forests, while providing economic and social benefits for the businesses and people that depend on them. The GFTN uses independent, multi-stakeholder based forest certification as a vital tool to apply the principles of responsible forest management and trade practices throughout the supply chain. The success of the GFTN can be seen as follows (as of April 2009):

Scope: represent 16% of all forest products traded internationally every year, with combined annual sales of $62 billion.

Represents: 187 trading deals with other GFTN participants.

Covers: with Forests over 21.5 million ha of certified forests and 12.2 million ha in progress to certification and with Trade covering 16% of the volume of internationally trade timber and fibre.

Employs: over 2.4 million people globally and supports 670 local families through community operations.

Whilst theoretically, there is enough wood in the world's forests to supply global wood requirements, an analysis carried out by WWF and the World Bank in 2001 indicated that by sustainably managing 60% of the world's forests, at different levels of intensity and for different purposes, the remaining 40% could be protected.

WWF therefore believes that by engaging organisations in challenging and innovative partnerships, companies can not only contribute to the sustainability of the planet, but to their own business viability and success. Through the GFTN, WWF works with the forest products industry to help it change the way it does business. The GFTN encourages trade links between companies committed to achieving responsible forestry and trade, and works to create those market conditions that support forest conservation, while providing economic and social benefits for the businesses and people that depend on them.

The GFTN provides a framework for companies; a proven "stepwise approach" which allows companies to develop forest management plans by outlining the various steps needed to achieve credible certification within an agreed timeframe. The GFTN also helps companies' phase-out products from unwanted timber sources and increase those from certified sources via this stepwise approach. WWF staff therefore provide local, on the ground support to ensure participating companies continuously improve their business practices. The GFTN has offices in 34 countries and engages with companies committed to responsible forest management and trade all around the world. (It will be noted here that there are more case studies that clearly detail the GFTN Green approach in "Green Supply Chains (2010). By WWF enabling the connections from End demand to the End supply; we can look at some of the lessons from these case studies.

Key Insights
The success of the GFTN is now being applied to other products like fish, palm oil and soya. Meanwhile what lessons for a Green supply chain are shown in the above case studies? We have summarized our view on these lessons below:
- General comments
- Need to change the way business is done
- Modern sustainable green practices work better than the previously used traditional ones

- Success comes from both the sustainability contributions, plus, the business viability and success, for example, the benefits to reputations by having full knowledge on the sourcing of products
- Supply chains do not change overnight

Approach used
- Facilitator for trade linking
- Challenging and innovative partnerships
- A proven stepwise approach with local on the ground support
- Independent multi-stakeholder based certification; this being seen as a vital and efficient tool to apply the green principles

Demand side needs
- The right demand market conditions
- Encouragement of major buyers, who in turn are pushed by environmental groups, public concern and pressure from shareholders who require up and running environmental and ethical companies to invest in

Supply side aspects
- Start with the leading producers
- Provide suppliers and others that depend on the supplier, with the economic and social benefits
- Increased costs of supply must be paid for by increased selling prices, though there are often cost savings from simplifying supply chains

– *Green Supply Chains – an action manifesto*, 2010, by Emmett and Sood

Appendix 3: The 4 Steps to SRM

This is not a "one size fits all" tool and we have already pointed out the real and too common dangers of looking for "quick fixes" by just using tools.

However, we do provide a guide on what needs to be done as the steps give a structure that will need thinking over with creative action.

It therefore requires iteration/looping and alignment with your specific and possibly unique circumstances.

After all, tools like this are not so much about giving answers, but more about raising questions and flexing with personal contextual applications.

With these comments in mind, the 4 structured steps are:
1. Where are we now, "Analyse the Current Performance"
2. Where do we want to be, "Objectives & Benefits"
3. How do we get there, "Practical Doing"
4. How do we know we have arrived, "Review & Check"

1. Where are we now? Analyse the Current performance

1.1 Where are we now? Questions we need to ask:

1.1.1 Start with some basic fact finding and expansive thinking:
- Who are the key stakeholders?
- What key issues and problems do we have?
- Who are the suppliers?
- Do we have basic supplier profiles; including size, spend, service and contact data?
- What do suppliers expect and need from us?

- How well are we meeting suppliers' expectations?
- How to provide supplier care and follow up?
- What needs to be done to make improvements?
- What are the barriers to making these improvements?
- How can we remove these barriers?
- Who currently controls the supplier relationship in our organisation?
- What will be the scope of the program?
- What confidentially agreements will we need e.g. to protect IP and rights?
- Will the program get top management commitment?

1.1.2. What resources are needed?

1.1.3. Will our culture support continuous improvement?

1.1.4. What are the perceived benefits/challenges of the program:
- List your 5 benefits
- List your 5 drawbacks

1.1.5. Do we recognise the core concepts are:
- Suppliers as assets/partners
- Long Term & HOT (honest, open, truthful) relationships
- Total cost analysis (TAC/TCO)

1.1.6. Do we see "It is a Continual Journey to a Destination" starting out with "Courtship > Engagement > Commitment"

1.2. Where are we now? To Do:

1.2.1. Rank suppliers by:
- Criticality/Risk

- Volume of spend
- Supplier capability
- For example:
  - Tactical/other suppliers and routine purchases in Kraljic's classification (see below)
  - Approved/preferred suppliers and leverage purchases in Kraljic's classification
  - Key suppliers and bottleneck purchases in Kraljic's classification
  - Strategic suppliers and critical purchases in Kraljic's classification

---

Kraljic's Purchase portfolio classification

Routine items: Routine buying of commodities, needing efficiency. Relationships maybe conducted at "arms length" for those low value items required irregularly.

Bottleneck items: Need here is to ensure the supply and reduce the risk on non supply and disruption to the business. Search for alternatives products/services whilst ensure can work with current supplier

Leverage items are those where a high volume is purchased. Here therefore the need is to obtain at the lowest cost.

Critical items require closer relationships to ensure competitive advantage is maintained. These will involve longer term relationships and partnering approaches with suppliers

---

1.2.2. Develop a sales pitch for SRM to use with internal stakeholders and key suppliers

1.2.3. Be ready to form a cross functional team

1.2.4. Create a stakeholder management plan

1.2.5. Develop a project timescale

1.2.6. Determine a communication plan

1.2.7. Define roles/responsibilities (RACI)

1.2.8. Confirm initial scope

1.2.9. Start to engage stakeholders and gain support

1.2.10. Make a formal business case that covers the following:
- SRM objectives, timelines, key stakeholders
- Current SRM readiness
- Challenges
- Benefits
- Short and long term SRM objectives
- "What does good look like" e.g. evidence of success and lessons from others experiences
- Financial requirements and ROI

2. Where do we want to be? Objectives & Benefits

2.1 Where do we want to be? Questions to ask ourselves:

2.1.1. Starting with basic facts to check against our formal business case:
- Can supplies be a source of competitive advantage (and not all will be)?
- Are strategic supplier relationships important to us (they should be some that are, but not all)?
- Will we use total costing approaches (TAC/TCO)?
- Are we prepared to be more responsive to our suppliers?
- Are we prepared to treat suppliers as collaborative partners?
- In 3 years, will existing suppliers be able to meet all our requirements?
- What are our precise expectations?

An example of where we may want to be is to "Achieve Strategic and Operational Excellence". For many this will also involve:

- Improve Revenue Generation by exploring opportunities to drive more revenue with 'quid pro quo' arrangements put in place
- Develop Innovative ideas through workshops and structured thinking

2.2 Where are we now? To do:

2.2.1 Review 2.1.1 above

2.2.2. Finalise 2.2.1 above with a clear statement of objectives and expected benefits

3. How do we get there? Practical doing with New Processes and Structures

3.1 How do we get there; Questions to ask ourselves:

3.1.1. Contract Hygiene and Awareness
- Is there a contract?
- Is it still fit for purpose?
- What needs to change? For example with the contract, "Usually in this business, the contract tells you what to do when things go wrong, but our contract tells you what to do to make things go right" (see the *Heathrow T5* Case Study)

3.1.2. Operational Performance
- Is the product/service being received acceptable; for example on quality, quantity, time, place, cost and other KPIs?
- Is there room for improvement?
- Determine the expected performance criteria

3.1.3. Power Dependency
- Who is really in control of the relationship, the customer or supplier?

- Do the perceptions "line up"?

3.1.4. Supplier and Power

- Do we really understand the Suppliers needs and expectations?
- What does the history/experience (own and others) tell us?
- What does the Supplier think of the Customer?

3.1.5. Power and Relationships

- Who else might influence the relationship and how should these people be managed?
- The following will assist in viewing power and relationships

---

Power

With buyer dominant

Small number of big buyers

Buy large percentage of a sellers output

Easy for buyer to switch

Many sources of supply

Low transaction costs

"Take it or leave it"

With seller dominant

Small number of big sellers

Supply to many buyers

Difficult for buyers to switch

Few sources of supply

High transaction costs

"Enforce"

Supplier Perception: Supplier Management Behaviours and Variations in relationships

Types of Relationships:

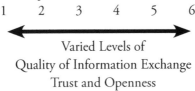

| 1 | 2 | 3 | 4 | 5 | 6 |

Varied Levels of
Quality of Information Exchange
Trust and Openness

Tactical	**Strategic**
Distant	Closer
"Deal for me"	In it together "we"
Shorter term	Longer Term
Level 1 Trust (Contractual)	Level 3 Trust (Goodwill)

Types of Relationships
Tactical
1. Adversary
"Take it or leave it"
2. Transactional
Normal ordering
3. Single Source
Exclusive agreements usually at fixed price for a specific time

Strategic
4. Strategic alliance
Working together for a specific purpose
5. Partnership
Commitment with shared risks/benefits
6. Co-destiny
Interdependency

Supply Chain Relationships: Relationship "Extremes"
More Tactical
- Trust based on what the contract says
- Personal relationships are not needed
- Strong use of ploys
- Price orientation
- Short term
- Measure by non compliance

More Strategic
- Goodwill trust and cooperation
- Strong personal relationship
- Mutual gains "rule"
- Total Cost of Ownership orientation
- Long term
- Both measure and agree remedial action

3.1.6. SRM Capability
- How well equipped and balanced is the SR Manager?

3.1.7. Executive support
- How do we get such sponsorship/support?
- Once SRM is running, how will we provide regular feedback?

3.1.8. Risk Assessment
- Have we undertaken a full review of supplier solvency, ICT security and corporate responsibility profiles?
- How will we maintain such reviews?

3.1.9. Formal Meeting Governance
- Have we formally scheduled Operational, Relationship and Strategic meetings?

3.1.10. Have we also considered:
- How trust will be developed?
- What training is needed for us and for suppliers?
- If we need a "best" supplier award?
- How will we be consistent in all of our approaches?
- How will we get supplier feedback? See the earlier Supplier Feedback 10 rules

3.2 How do we get there? To Do:

3.2.1. Supplier Account Planning
- Develop agreements on what the 30/90/180 day activities are to be

3.2.2. Other possibilities to consider using are:
- Alliance structures
- Parallel sourcing
- VA/VE (Value analysis/engineering)
- Supplier development
- Study groups

3.2 3. Check on the multi disciplinary project team
- (E.g. 1 Senior Manager along with Purchase – Production – Distribution Logistics – Marketing) has explored the following:
- Is the remit agreed and clear?
- Who is to be involved/consulted?
- What are the core values of the SRM program?
- Does this fit with the current company culture?
- How will we evaluate suppliers?
- What resources are needed for this programme?
- How will effective communications be developed?

3.2.4. Format an Action Plan and document the process (Written Document) both for Internal & External:

- Develop the Mission Statement
- Quantify the Objectives
- Detail Resources & Responsibilities
- Implementation mechanisms
- Project team future
- Statement of Principles
- Start date(s)
- Guard against "one size fits all" approaches
  (With this step on document the process, it can be usefully noted that ICT departments do often have good process and governance, as they were early users of suppliers/ outsourcing).

3.2 5. Use the correct ICT

- Supplier performance management and contract management systems should be common
- Best models usually come from CRM sales based systems that are reversed into procurement, for example, customer service becomes supplier service
- Ensure you are not using ICT for its own sake

3.2.6. Up skill people

- Suppliers have full time key account managers but too often, procurement/supply chain actually see SRM as being an add on
- Also be aware that, Buyers are often seen and perceived as being "table thumpers" and having only a "low cost only" interest = not appropriate behaviour for good relationships

3.2.7 "Sign off" and go ahead.

4. How do we know we have arrived? Review and check

4.1 How do we know we have arrived? To Do:

4.1.1. Measure the hard and soft benefits achieved
- SRM goes well beyond any Procurement Category Management approach, as whilst "hard" cost is reduced, there are infinitive increased value opportunities in SRM. For example, cost reductions from those "soft" benefits like better sharing, communications, relationships, fairness etc.

4.1.2. Improvement Reporting
- Key improvement reporting (tracking the whole SRM programme) should be established

4.1.3. Risks & Issues
- Formal tracking of key risks and issues should take place
- For example, have we achieved the appropriate behavioural change, or, is there still more to do?

4.1 4. SRM Training
- Development of SR Managers should continue

4.1.5. Benefits Assessment and Planning
- Given the application of 1-4 above and the measurement and reporting of benefits (be they financial or more intangible, i.e. service improvements, employee engagement etc.), these should all continue to be tracked and/or forecast.

And finally, building the case for SRM

In general, SRM does not require significant incremental investment. Some key considerations are:

- Consider whether your organisation needs a return on investment-based approach or whether it has philosophically bought into the value that SRM can deliver.
- Review all savings delivered historically to identify existing delivery from SRM. This reached 80% at one organisation.
- Estimate the costs and issues incurred that could have been avoided if more resources had been dedicated to managing relationships.
- Start small and build the case for investment. One organisation built savings delivery from £20 million in year one to $350 million in year four, with significant revenue benefits on top.
- Consider setting a target for post-contract savings, with one per cent used by one organisation. This generated an ROI of 100:1 and increased dedicated SRM resources from 2 to 23.
- Invest effort in tracking and recording all benefits targeted and delivered, both quantitative and qualitative. Qualitative stories capture executive attention.
- Work with finance to ensure a full range of benefits gets captured in the benefit-tracking tool. Make links to business metrics wherever possible.

  – Webb and Hughes, in *CPO Agenda*, Autumn 2009.

7 Bibliography

Christopher, M. (1998). *Logistics and Supply Chain Management*, Prentice Hall.

Covey, S.M.R. (2006). *The Speed of Trust*, Simon & Schuster.

Cordon, T. & Vollmann, C. (2008). *The Power of Two*, Palgrave Macmillan.

Carlzon, J. (1987). *Moments of Truth*, Harper Paperbacks.

Day, Alan. (2010). *SRM Report*, State of Flux.

Emmett, S. and Crocker, B. (2006). *The Relationship Driven Supply Chain*, Gower.

Emmett, S. and Crocker, B. (2008). *Excellence in Procurement*, Cambridge Academic.

Emmett, S. and Crocker, B. (2008). *Excellence in Supplier Management*, Cambridge Academic.

Emmett, S. and Sood, V. (2010). *Green Supply Chains*, Wiley.

Focus, February 1996, Chartered Institute of Logistics and Transport.

Focus, January 2011, Chartered Institute of Logistics and Transport.

Human Resources, November 2004.

IACCM, 24 February 2011, *Contracting Excellence* e-zine.

Institute of Business Ethics Report, 2006.

IJLR&A, June 2010, Volume 14, number 3.

Kouzes, James and Posner, Barry Z. (2012). *The Leadership Challenge*, Jossey Bass.

The Office of Government Commerce, (2006) *Supply Chain Management in the Public Sector-A Guide*.

The Audit Commission report. (1998). *A Fruitful Partnership*.

The Housing Forum report, (2003). *Partnering at Work*.

Logistics Manager, June 2004.

Logistics Manager, March 2008.
People Management, 22 February 2007.
Prime Contractor Handbook of Supply Chain Management, (March 1999). *Rethinking Construction.*
Sunday Times, 11 February 2007.
Supply Management, 6 October 2005. Chartered Institute of Purchasing and Supply.
Supply Management, 18 January 2007. Chartered Institute of Purchasing and Supply.
Supply Management, 18 March 2010. Chartered Institute of Purchasing and Supply
Supply Management, 1 January 2012. Chartered Institute of Purchasing and Supply.

www.instituteforcollaborativeworking.com
www.logic-oil.com
www.pilottaskforce.co.uk

Made in the USA
Columbia, SC
14 September 2017